Connected Mathematics

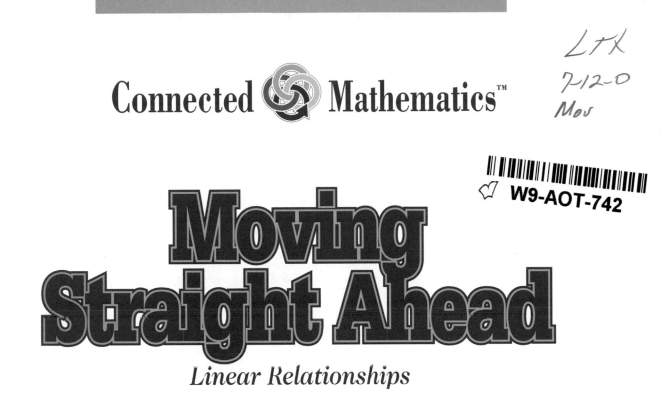

Moving Straight Ahead

Linear Relationships

Student Edition

Glenda Lappan
James T. Fey
William M. Fitzgerald
Susan N. Friel
Elizabeth Difanis Phillips

Developed at Michigan State University

DALE SEYMOUR PUBLICATIONS®
MENLO PARK, CALIFORNIA

Connected Mathematics™ was developed at Michigan State University with the support of National Science Foundation Grant No. MDR 9150217.

This project was supported, in part,
by the
National Science Foundation
Opinions expressed are those of the authors
and not necessarily those of the Foundation

The Michigan State University authors and administration have agreed that all MSU royalties arising from this publication will be devoted to purposes supported by the Department of Mathematics and the MSU Mathematics Education Enrichment Fund.

This book is published by Dale Seymour Publications®, an imprint of Addison Wesley Longman, Inc.

Dale Seymour Publications
2725 Sand Hill Road
Menlo Park, CA 94025
Customer Service: 800 872-1100

Managing Editor: Catherine Anderson
Project Editor: Stacey Miceli
Revision Editor: James P. McAuliffe
Production/Manufacturing Director: Janet Yearian
Production/Manufacturing Coordinators: Claire Flaherty, Alan Noyes
Design Manager: John F. Kelly
Photo Editor: Roberta Spieckerman
Design: PCI, San Antonio, TX
Composition: London Road Design, Palo Alto, CA
Electronic Prepress Revision: A. W. Kingston Publishing Services, Chandler, AZ
Illustrations: Pauline Phung, Margaret Copeland, Ray Godfrey
Cover: Ray Godfrey

Photo Acknowledgements: 8 © Gary S. Settles/Photo Researchers, Inc.; 15 © Alan Carey/The Image Works; 18 © Thelma Shumsky/The Image Works; 19 © Bob Daemmrich/The Image Works; 29 © Bob Martin/Allsport; 51 © Peter Southwick/Stock, Boston; 60 © Jack Dermid/Photo Researchers, Inc.; 65 © Daniel Wray/The Image Works; 75 © Zigy Kaluzny/Tony Stone Images; 88 Special Collections, California Academy of Science; © G. Goodwin/Superstock, Inc.

Order number 45836
ISBN 1-57232-641-7

4 5 6 7 8 9 10-BA-01 00 99

The Connected Mathematics Project Staff

Project Directors

James T. Fey
University of Maryland

William M. Fitzgerald
Michigan State University

Susan N. Friel
University of North Carolina at Chapel Hill

Glenda Lappan
Michigan State University

Elizabeth Difanis Phillips
Michigan State University

Project Manager

Kathy Burgis
Michigan State University

Technical Coordinator

Judith Martus Miller
Michigan State University

Curriculum Development Consultants

David Ben-Chaim
Weizmann Institute

Alex Friedlander
Weizmann Institute

Eleanor Geiger
University of Maryland

Jane Mitchell
University of North Carolina at Chapel Hill

Anthony D. Rickard
Alma College

Collaborating Teachers/Writers

Mary K. Bouck
Portland, Michigan

Jacqueline Stewart
Okemos, Michigan

Graduate Assistants

Scott J. Baldridge
Michigan State University

Angie S. Eshelman
Michigan State University

M. Faaiz Gierdien
Michigan State University

Jane M. Keiser
Indiana University

Angela S. Krebs
Michigan State University

James M. Larson
Michigan State University

Ronald Preston
Indiana University

Tat Ming Sze
Michigan State University

Sarah Theule-Lubienski
Michigan State University

Jeffrey J. Wanko
Michigan State University

Evaluation Team

Mark Hoover
Michigan State University

Diane V. Lambdin
Indiana University

Sandra K. Wilcox
Michigan State University

Judith S. Zawojewski
National-Louis University

Teacher/Assessment Team

Kathy Booth
Waverly, Michigan

Anita Clark
Marshall, Michigan

Julie Faulkner
Traverse City, Michigan

Theodore Gardella
Bloomfield Hills, Michigan

Yvonne Grant
Portland, Michigan

Linda R. Lobue
Vista, California

Suzanne McGrath
Chula Vista, California

Nancy McIntyre
Troy, Michigan

Mary Beth Schmitt
Traverse City, Michigan

Linda Walker
Tallahassee, Florida

Software Developer

Richard Burgis
East Lansing, Michigan

Development Center Directors

Nicholas Branca
San Diego State University

Dianne Briars
Pittsburgh Public Schools

Frances R. Curcio
New York University

Perry Lanier
Michigan State University

J. Michael Shaughnessy
Portland State University

Charles Vonder Embse
Central Michigan University

Special thanks to the students and teachers at these pilot schools!

Baker Demonstration School
Evanston, Illinois

Bertha Vos Elementary School
Traverse City, Michigan

Blair Elementary School
Traverse City, Michigan

Bloomfield Hills Middle School
Bloomfield Hills, Michigan

Brownell Elementary School
Flint, Michigan

Catlin Gabel School
Portland, Oregon

Cherry Knoll Elementary School
Traverse City, Michigan

Cobb Middle School
Tallahassee, Florida

Courtade Elementary School
Traverse City, Michigan

Duke School for Children
Durham, North Carolina

DeVeaux Junior High School
Toledo, Ohio

East Junior High School
Traverse City, Michigan

Eastern Elementary School
Traverse City, Michigan

Eastlake Elementary School
Chula Vista, California

Eastwood Elementary School
Sturgis, Michigan

Elizabeth City Middle School
Elizabeth City, North Carolina

Franklinton Elementary School
Franklinton, North Carolina

Frick International Studies Academy
Pittsburgh, Pennsylvania

Gundry Elementary School
Flint, Michigan

Hawkins Elementary School
Toledo, Ohio

Hilltop Middle School
Chula Vista, California

Holmes Middle School
Flint, Michigan

Interlochen Elementary School
Traverse City, Michigan

Los Altos Elementary School
San Diego, California

Louis Armstrong Middle School
East Elmhurst, New York

McTigue Junior High School
Toledo, Ohio

National City Middle School
National City, California

Norris Elementary School
Traverse City, Michigan

Northeast Middle School
Minneapolis, Minnesota

Oak Park Elementary School
Traverse City, Michigan

Old Mission Elementary School
Traverse City, Michigan

Old Orchard Elementary School
Toledo, Ohio

Portland Middle School
Portland, Michigan

Reizenstein Middle School
Pittsburgh, Pennsylvania

Sabin Elementary School
Traverse City, Michigan

Shepherd Middle School
Shepherd, Michigan

Sturgis Middle School
Sturgis, Michigan

Terrell Lane Middle School
Louisburg, North Carolina

Tierra del Sol Middle School
Lakeside, California

Traverse Heights Elementary School
Traverse City, Michigan

University Preparatory Academy
Seattle, Washington

Washington Middle School
Vista, California

Waverly East Intermediate School
Lansing, Michigan

Waverly Middle School
Lansing, Michigan

West Junior High School
Traverse City, Michigan

Willow Hill Elementary School
Traverse City, Michigan

Contents

Moving Straight Ahead

Henri challenges his older brother Emile to a walking race. Emile figures out that his walking rate is 2.5 meters per second, and Henri's walking rate is 1 meter per second. Emile agrees to give Henri a 45-meter head start. Emile knows Henri would enjoy winning the race, but he does not want to make the race so short that it is obvious his brother will win. What distance would allow Henri to win in a close race?

Rosa's grandfather gives her some money as a birthday gift. She plans to put her birthday money in a safe place and add the same amount from her allowance to it each week. After five weeks, she will have a total of $175, and after eight weeks, she will have $190. How much money is Rosa planning to save each week? How much money did her grandfather give her for her birthday?

To estimate the outside temperature, count cricket chirps. If a cricket chirps n times in one minute, then the temperature, t, in degrees Fahrenheit can be computed with the formula $t = \frac{1}{4}n + 40$. What is the temperature if a cricket chirps 150 times in a minute?

In *Variables and Patterns*, you investigated relationships between variables. You displayed relationships as tables, graphs, and equations. Some of the graphs you made—such as the graph of distance and time for a van traveling at a steady rate—were straight lines. Relationships with graphs that are straight lines are called *linear relationships*. In this unit, you will study linear relationships.

You will learn about the characteristics of a linear relationship, and you will see how you can determine whether a relationship is linear by looking at its equation or a table of values.

As you work on the investigations in this unit, you will use what you are learning about linear relationships to answer interesting questions like those on the previous page.

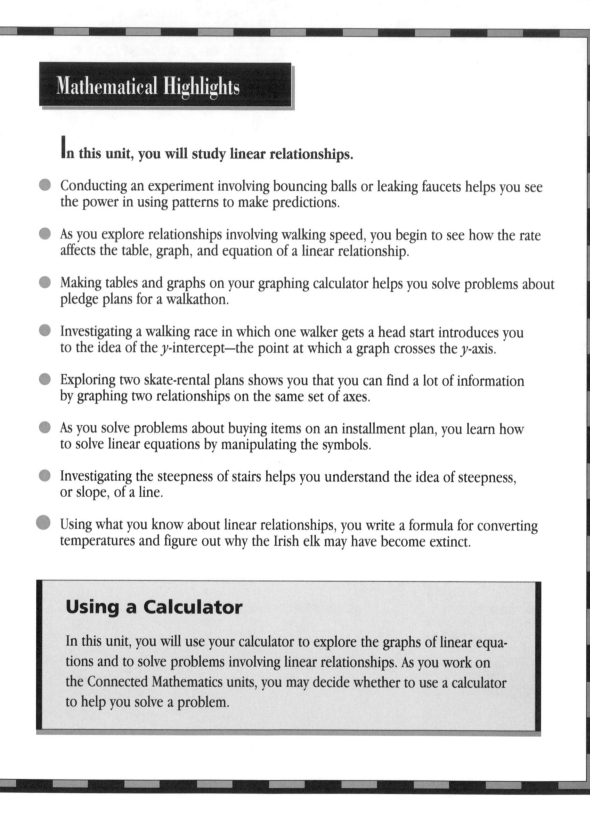

Mathematical Highlights

In this unit, you will study linear relationships.

● Conducting an experiment involving bouncing balls or leaking faucets helps you see the power in using patterns to make predictions.

● As you explore relationships involving walking speed, you begin to see how the rate affects the table, graph, and equation of a linear relationship.

● Making tables and graphs on your graphing calculator helps you solve problems about pledge plans for a walkathon.

● Investigating a walking race in which one walker gets a head start introduces you to the idea of the *y*-intercept—the point at which a graph crosses the *y*-axis.

● Exploring two skate-rental plans shows you that you can find a lot of information by graphing two relationships on the same set of axes.

● As you solve problems about buying items on an installment plan, you learn how to solve linear equations by manipulating the symbols.

● Investigating the steepness of stairs helps you understand the idea of steepness, or slope, of a line.

● Using what you know about linear relationships, you write a formula for converting temperatures and figure out why the Irish elk may have become extinct.

Using a Calculator

In this unit, you will use your calculator to explore the graphs of linear equations and to solve problems involving linear relationships. As you work on the Connected Mathematics units, you may decide whether to use a calculator to help you solve a problem.

Predicting from Patterns

All around you, things occur in patterns. Once you observe a pattern, you can predict information beyond and between the data observed. The ability to use patterns to make predictions makes it possible for you to run to the right position to catch a fly ball or to guess how a story will end. Often, you are not even aware that you are thinking about patterns until something surprises you because it does not fit a familiar pattern. For example, the first time you bounced a superball, you may have had trouble catching it because you weren't expecting it to bounce so high. You were basing your expectations on patterns you had observed for other types of balls.

In many situations, patterns become apparent only after sufficient data are collected, organized, and displayed. In this investigation, you will conduct an experiment and use patterns in the data to make predictions.

1.1 Conducting an Experiment

Problems 1.1A and 1.1B are experiments. Your group should carry out *only one* of these experiments. Read the directions carefully *before you start.* Be prepared to explain your findings to the rest of the class.

- In Problem 1.1A, you investigate the rate at which a leaking faucet loses water.
- In Problem 1.1B, you investigate how the drop height of a ball is related to its bounce height.

1.1A: Wasting Water

In this experiment, you will simulate a leaking faucet and collect data about the volume of water lost at 5-second intervals. You will then use the patterns in your results to predict how much water is wasted when a faucet leaks for one month.

Equipment: a paper cup, water, a sharp object (such as a paper clip or a small nail), a clear measuring container, and a watch or clock with a second hand

Directions: You will need to figure out how to divide the work among the members of your group.

1. Make a table with columns for recording time and amount of water lost. Fill in the time column with values from 0 seconds to 60 seconds in 5-second intervals (that is, 5, 10, 15, and so on).

2. Use the sharp object to punch a small hole in the bottom of the cup. Cover the hole with your finger.
3. Fill the paper cup with water.
4. Hold the paper cup over the measuring container.
5. When you are ready to begin timing, uncover the hole so that the water drips into the measuring container.

6. In a table, record the amount of water in the measuring container at 5-second intervals, up to a total time of 60 seconds.

Problem 1.1A

A. Make a coordinate graph of the data you collected.

B. What variables did you investigate in this experiment? Describe the relationship between the variables.

C. If a faucet dripped at the same rate as your cup does, how much water would be wasted in 2 minutes? In 2.5 minutes? In 3 minutes and 15 seconds? Explain how you made your predictions. Did you use the table, the graph, or some other method? What clues in the data helped you?

■ Problem 1.1A Follow-Up

1. If a faucet dripped into the measuring container at the same rate as your paper cup does, how long would it take for the container to overflow?
2. Besides time, what other variables affect the amount of water in the measuring container?
3. If a faucet leaked at the same rate as your paper cup, how much water would be wasted in one month? Explain how you arrived at your answer.
4. Find out how much water costs in your area. Use this information and your answer from question 3 to figure out the cost of the water wasted by a leaking faucet in one month.

1.1B: Bouncing Balls

You have probably bounced lots of kinds of balls. After bouncing a ball many times, you are better able to predict its behavior. For example, practicing bouncing a basketball can help you make a more accurate bounce pass in a game. In this experiment, you will investigate how the height from which a ball is dropped is related to the height it bounces.

Equipment: a meterstick and a ball that bounces

Directions: You will need to figure out how to divide up the work among the members of your group.

1. Make a table with columns for recording drop height and bounce height.
2. Hold the meterstick perpendicular to a flat surface, such as an uncarpeted floor, a table, or a desk.
3. Choose and record a height on the meterstick as the height from which you will drop the ball. Hold the ball at this height.
4. *Drop* the ball, and record the height of the first bounce. (You may have to do this several times before you feel confident you can make a good estimate of the bounce height.)
5. Repeat this for several different drop heights.

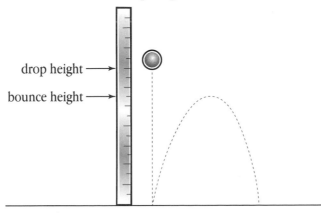

Problem 1.1B

A. Make a coordinate graph of the data you collected.

B. What variables did you investigate in this experiment? Describe the relationship between the variables.

C. Predict the bounce height for a drop height of 2 meters. Explain how you made your prediction. Did you use the table, the graph, or some other method? What clues in the data helped you?

D. Predict the drop height needed for a bounce height of 2 meters. Explain how you made your prediction. Did you use the table, the graph, or some other method? What clues in the data helped you?

E. What bounce height would you expect for a drop height of 0 centimeters? Where would this be on the graph?

■ **Problem 1.1B Follow-Up**

Besides the drop height, what other variables affect the bounce height of the ball?

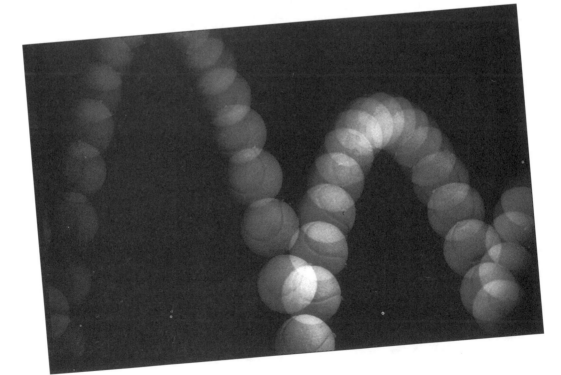

As you work on these ACE questions, use your calculator whenever you need it.

Applications

1. The table of data below was produced by students who did the bouncing-ball experiment.

Drop height (centimeters)	20	30	40	50	60	70	80
Bounce height (centimeters)	10	18	25	32	38	45	50

   a. Make a coordinate graph of these data.

   b. Predict the bounce height for a drop height of 45 centimeters. What method did you use to make your prediction?

   c. Predict the bounce height for a drop height of 140 centimeters.

   d. Predict the drop height needed for a bounce height of 60 centimeters.

   e. Are you equally confident about each prediction you made in parts b–d? Explain.

2. The table of data below was produced by students who did the leaking-faucet experiment. The measuring container they used held only 100 milliliters. If the students had continued their experiment, after how many seconds would the measuring container have overflowed?

Time (seconds)	10	20	30	40	50	60	70
Water loss (milliliters)	2	5	8.5	11.5	14	16.5	19.5

3. **a.** Think of two variables whose relationship can be represented by a straight-line graph like the one at the right. Copy the graph, and add labels for the variables you chose.

   b. Make up a question about your variables that could be answered by using the graph.

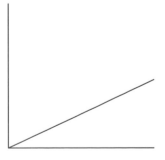

Connections

4. In *Variables and Patterns,* you saw that the distance traveled by the tour van depended on time. Suppose the van averaged a steady 60 miles per hour on the interstate highway. The table below shows the relationship between the time traveled and the distance.

Time (hours)	0.5	1.0	1.5	2.0	2.5	3.0	3.5
Distance (miles)	30	60					

a. Copy and complete the table.

b. Make a coordinate graph of the data in the table.

c. Write a rule that describes the relationship between distance and time.

d. Predict the distance traveled in 8 hours.

e. Predict the time needed to travel 300 miles.

f. Pick a pair of (time, distance) values from the table. How is the pair related to the graph and the rule?

5. The soccer boosters make $5 on each T-shirt they sell. This can be described by the equation $A = 5n$, where A is the amount of money made and n is the number of T-shirts sold.

a. Make a table and a graph showing the amount of money made by selling up to ten T-shirts.

b. Compare the table and the graph from part a with the table and the graph you made for your experiment in Problem 1.1A or 1.1B. How are the tables similar? How are they different? How are the graphs similar? How are they different? What do you think causes the similarities and differences?

c. Compare the table, graph, and rule for the T-shirt sale with the table, graph, and rule in question 4. Describe the similarities and differences.

6. Denise and Takashi worked together on the leaking-faucet experiment. Each of them made a graph of the data they collected. What might have caused their graphs to look so different?

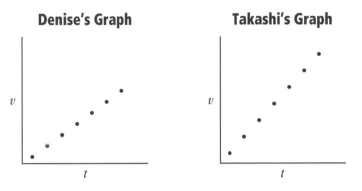

Denise's Graph   **Takashi's Graph**

7. What might the following graph mean with regard to the leaking-faucet experiment?

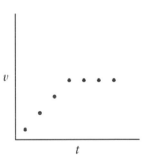

8. Jack does the bouncing-ball experiment and collects the following data.

Drop height (centimeters)	30	40	50	60	70	80	90
Bounce height (centimeters)	20	24	31	37	43	51	60

Jack says he does not need to make a graph to predict the bounce height for a drop height of 130 centimeters. He says the rule is that the bounce height is always two thirds of the drop height. Is his rule reasonable? Explain.

Extensions

9. Mr. Delgrosso's class conducted an experiment using a spring and some weights. They placed each weight on the end of the spring and measured the length of the stretched spring.

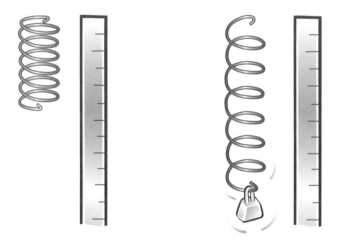

a. One student made the graph below to display the class's data from the experiment. What are the variables? Describe the general relationship between the variables.

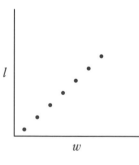

b. Another student used the same data to make the graph below. How is this graph different from the graph in part a? Is it possible that both graphs are correct? Explain.

Mathematical Reflections

In this investigation, you conducted an experiment. By organizing your data into a table and a graph, you observed patterns and used the patterns to make predictions. These questions will help you summarize what you have learned:

1. One of the goals of this unit is to discover ways to identify a linear relationship from its table. Look at the table you made for your experiment and the tables you have made for other straight-line relationships. What do you think characterizes the table of a linear relationship?

2. What other relationships that you have investigated, in this class or somewhere else, do you now suspect to be linear?

Think about your answers to these questions, discuss your ideas with other students and your teacher, and then write a summary of your findings in your journal.

Walking Rates

In *Variables and Patterns,* you read about five college students who set up a bicycle-touring business. The students used tables, graphs, and equations to look for patterns relating variables such as cost, income, and profit.

For example, the total cost to rent bikes depends on the number of people on the tour. We say that the rental cost is a *function of* the number of people on the tour. The variables in this situation are the number of people and the cost. If you were interested in how these variables are related, you might ask questions like these:

As the number of people on the tour increases, what happens to the cost to rent the bikes?

If the tour partners want to decrease the cost of renting bikes, how will this affect the number of people who can go on the tour?

For example, one bike shop charges $300 plus $20 per bike to rent bikes for one week. If we let C be the total cost to rent the bikes and n the number of people who go on the tour, we can write this equation to show the relationship between the number of people on the tour and the total rental cost:

$$C = 300 + 20n$$

Remember that $20n$ means 20 *times n.* If a variable is multiplied by a number, we can omit the times sign.

In *Variables and Patterns,* you also looked at the number of miles a van covers in a specified period of time. For example, if a van averages 60 miles per hour, then the distance covered depends on the number of hours the van travels. In other words, the distance is a *function of* the number of hours of travel. The variables are distance traveled and time. The relationship between these variables can be expressed as

$$d = 60t$$

where d represents the distance traveled in miles and t represents the time in hours.

The graphs of $C = 300 + 20n$ and $d = 60t$ are straight lines.

Rental Costs

Van Distances

From the graphs, it is easy to see that the relationships between the number of bikes and the rental cost, and between the miles traveled and the time are **linear relationships**. In this investigation, you will consider this question:

> *How can you determine whether a situation is linear by examining a table of data or an equation?*

Once you have determined—from the table, the graph, or the equation—that a relationship is linear, you can explore this question:

> *How does changing one of the quantities in a situation affect the table, the graph, or the equation?*

For example, how does changing the cost per bike affect the table, the graph, and the equation of the relationship between the number of customers and the total rental cost? How does increasing the average speed at which the van travels affect the table, the graph, and the equation of the relationship between distance and time?

2.1 Walking to the Yogurt Shop

Mr. Goldberg's gym class does an experiment to determine their walking rates. Here are the results for three students.

Name	Walking rate
Terry	1 meter per second
Jade	2 meters per second
Jerome	2.5 meters per second

Jerome wonders how a person's walking rate would affect the amount of time it takes him or her to walk from school to the frozen yogurt shop.

Problem 2.1

A. If Terry, Jade, and Jerome leave school together and walk toward the frozen yogurt shop at the rates given in the table, how far apart will they be after 1 minute?

B. If the yogurt shop is 750 meters from school, how long will it take each student to walk there?

C. When Jerome arrives at the yogurt shop, how far away will Terry be?

■ Problem 2.1 Follow-Up

1. In Problem 2.1, what strategies did you use to get your answers?

2. Does Problem 2.1 involve linear relationships? Explain why or why not.

2.2 Changing the Walking Rate

In Problem 2.1, you saw that a person's walking rate determines the time it takes him or her to walk a given distance. In this problem, you will more closely examine the effect that walking rate has on the relationship between time and distance walked. Your findings will give you some important clues about how to identify linear relationships from tables, graphs, and equations.

Problem 2.2

A. In Problem 2.1, each student walked at a different rate. Use the walking rates given in that problem to make a table showing the distance walked by each student after different numbers of seconds. How does the walking rate affect the data in the table?

Time (seconds)	Distance (meters)		
	Terry	Jade	Jerome
0	0	0	0
1	1	2	2.5
2			
3			
.			
.			
.			

B. Graph the time and distance data for the three students on the same coordinate axes. Use a different color for each student's data. How does the walking rate affect the graphs?

C. For each student, write an equation that gives the relationship between the time and the distance walked. Let d represent the distance in meters and t represent the time in seconds. How does the walking rate affect the equations?

■ Problem 2.2 Follow-Up

While reading a sports magazine, Abby finds the following time and distance data for an athlete in an Olympic race. She wonders whether the data represent a linear relationship. Abby knows that if the relationship is linear, the data will lie on a straight line when graphed.

Time (seconds)	Distance (meters)
0	0
1	2
2	4
3	8
4	13
5	17

1. Use the table to determine how the distance changes as the time increases. How can you use this information to predict whether or not the data will lie on a straight line when graphed?

2. Describe the race that might have produced these data.

2.3 Walking for Charity

Ms. Chang's class decides to participate in a walkathon to raise money for a local hospital. Each participant in the walkathon must find sponsors to pledge a certain amount of money for each mile the participant walks.

Ms. Chang says that some sponsors might ask the students to suggest a pledge amount. The class wants to agree on how much they will ask for. Leanne says that $1 per mile would be appropriate. Gilberto says that $2 per mile would be better because it would bring in more money. Alana points out that if they ask for too much money, not as many people will want to be sponsors. She suggests that they ask each sponsor for a $5 donation plus 50¢ per mile.

Problem 2.3

In this problem, we will refer to Leanne, Gilberto, and Alana's suggestions as pledge plans.

A. 1. Make a table showing the amount of money a sponsor would owe under each pledge plan if a student walked distances between 0 and 10 miles.

2. Graph the three pledge plans on the same coordinate axes. Use a different color for each plan.

3. For each pledge plan, write an equation that can be used to calculate the amount of money a sponsor owes, given the total distance the student walks.

B. What effect does increasing the amount pledged per mile have on the table? On the graph? On the equation?

C. If a student walks 8 miles in the walkathon, how much would a sponsor owe under each pledge plan? Explain how you got your answer.

D. For a sponsor to owe a student $10, how many miles would the student have to walk under each pledge plan? Explain how you got your answer.

E. Alana suggested that each sponsor make a $5 donation and then pledge 50¢ per mile. How is this fixed $5 donation represented in the table? In the graph? In the equation?

■ Problem 2.3 Follow-Up

1. a. On the graph of a pledge plan, the point (2, 6) means that a student who walks 2 miles earns $6 from each sponsor. On which of the graphs is the point (2, 6)?

b. Find a point on each graph, and describe what the coordinates of the point mean in the context of the walkathon.

2. a. Write an equation for a pledge plan whose graph is a steeper line than any of the lines you graphed in the problem. Check your equation by graphing it on the coordinate axes with the other three lines.

b. Write an equation for a pledge plan whose graph is less steep than any of the lines you graphed in the problem. Check your equation by graphing it on the coordinate axes with the other lines.

2.4 Walking to Win

In Mr. Goldberg's gym class, Emile finds out that his walking rate is 2.5 meters per second. When he gets home from school, he times his little brother Henri, as Henri walks 100 meters. He figures out that Henri's walking rate is 1 meter per second.

Henri challenges Emile to a walking race. Because Emile's walking rate is faster, Emile gives Henri a 45-meter head start.

Problem 2.4

Emile knows his brother would enjoy winning the race, but he does not want to make the race so short that it is obvious his brother will win.

What would be a good distance to make the race so that Henri will win in a close race? Describe your strategy, and give evidence to support your answer.

■ Problem 2.4 Follow-Up

What would be a good distance to choose if Emile wants to beat his brother but wants the race to be close? Explain.

2.5 Crossing the Line

In Problem 2.4, there are many strategies you can use to determine a good distance for the race. Some strategies are more efficient or useful than others. Here are three powerful ways to tackle the problem:

1. Make a table showing time and distance data for both brothers.
2. On the same set of axes, graph time and distance data for both brothers.
3. Write an equation for each brother showing the relationship between the time and the distance from the starting line.

Problem 2.5

Use the information from Problem 2.4.

A. 1. Make a table showing the distance each brother is from the starting line at several different times during the first 40 seconds.

2. On the same set of axes, graph the time and the distance from the starting line for both brothers.

3. Write an equation for each brother showing the relationship between the time and the distance from the starting line.

B. How far from the starting line will Emile overtake Henri? Explain how you can use the table and the graph to answer this question.

C. After how many seconds will Emile overtake Henri? Explain how you can use the table and the graph to answer this question.

■ **Problem 2.5 Follow-Up**

1. After 3 seconds, who will be ahead? By how much?
2. How far will Henri be from the starting line when Emile has walked 10 meters?
3. a. Which graph is steeper?
   b. How can you determine which of two lines will be steeper from their tables? From their equations?
4. Explain how you can use the table, the graph, and the equations to determine how far from the starting line each brother will be after 5 minutes.
5. a. At what points do Emile's and Henri's graphs cross the y-axis? What do these points mean in terms of the race?
   b. How can you predict where a graph will cross the y-axis from a table? From an equation?

6. Emile's friend Yvette joins the race. Yvette has a head start of 20 meters and walks at 2 meters per second.

    a. Copy and complete the table below to show Yvette's distance from the starting line for 0 to 7 seconds.

Time (seconds)	Distance (meters)
0	20
1	
2	
3	
4	
5	
6	
7	

    b. Which of the following equations gives the relationship between Yvette's distance from the starting line, d, and the time, t?

      i. $d = 20 + 2t$

      ii. $d = 2 + 20$

      iii. $d = 20t + 2$

      iv. $d = 20 + t$

      v. none of the above

As you work on these ACE questions, use your calculator whenever you need it.

Applications

In 1–3, use the following information: José, Mario, and Melanie went on a weeklong cycling trip. The table below gives the distance each person traveled for the first 3 hours of the trip. The table shows only the time when the riders were actually biking, not when they stopped to rest, eat, and so on.

	Distance (miles)		
Cycling time (hours)	José	Mario	Melanie
0	0	0	0
1	5	7	9
2	10	14	18
3	15	21	27

1. a. How fast did each person travel for the first 3 hours? Explain how you got your answer.

b. Assume that each person continued at this rate. Find the distance each person traveled in 7 hours.

2. a. Graph the time and distance data for all three riders on the same coordinate axes.

b. Use the graphs to find the distance each person traveled in $6\frac{1}{2}$ hours.

c. Use the graphs to find the time it took each person to travel 70 miles.

d. How does the rate at which each person rides affect the graphs?

3. a. For each rider, write an equation that can be used to calculate the distance traveled after a given number of hours.

b. Use your equations from part a to calculate the distance each person traveled in $6\frac{1}{2}$ hours.

c. How does a person's biking rate show up in his or her equation?

4. Mike was on the bike trip with José, Mario, and Melanie (from questions 1–3). He made the following table of the distances he traveled during day 1 of the trip.

Time (hours)	Distance (miles)
0	0
1	6.5
2	13
3	19.5
4	26
5	32.5
6	39

a. Assume Mike continued riding at this rate for the entire bike trip. Write an equation for the distance Mike traveled after t hours.

b. Sketch a graph of the equation.

c. When you made your graph, how did you choose the range of values for the time axis? For the distance axis?

d. How can you find the distance Mike traveled in 7 hours and in $9\frac{1}{2}$ hours, using the table? The graph? The equation?

e. How can you find the number of hours it took Mike to travel 100 miles and 237 miles, using the table? The graph? The equation?

f. For parts d and e, give the advantages and disadvantages of using each form of representation—a table, a graph, and an equation—to find the answers.

g. Compare the rate at which Mike rides with the rates at which José, Mario, and Melanie ride. Who rides the fastest? How can you determine this from the tables? From the graphs? From the equations?

5. Alicia was also on the bike trip. The distance she traveled in t hours is represented by this equation:

$$d = 7.5t$$

a. At what rate did Alicia travel?

b. If the graph of Alicia's distance and time were put on the same set of axes as Mike's graph, where would it be located in relationship to Mike's graph? Describe the location without actually making the graph.

c. If the graph of Alicia's distance and time were put on the same set of axes as José's, Mario's, and Melanie's graphs, where would it be located in relationship to the other graphs? Describe the location without actually making the graph.

6. The students in Ms. Chang's class decide to order T-shirts that advertise the walkathon. Miguel obtains two different quotes for the costs for the shirts.

One Size Fits All charges $4 per shirt.
You Draw It/We Print It charges $75 plus $3 per shirt.

a. For each company, write an equation Miguel could use to calculate the cost for any number of shirts.

b. On the same set of axes, graph both equations from part a.

c. Which company do you think the class should buy shirts from? What factors influenced your decision?

d. For what number of T-shirts is the cost the same for both companies? Explain how you got your answer.

In 7–9, refer to tables a–c.

a.

x	y
−2	3
−1	3
0	3
1	3
2	3
3	3

b.

x	y
−3	9
−2	4
−1	1
0	0
1	1
2	4

c.

x	y
0	0
2	−4
3	−8
4	−12
8	−16

7. How are the patterns in tables a–c similar? How are they different?

8. Make a graph of the data in each table.

9. Which tables represent a linear relationship? Explain how you decided.

10. The equation $C = 10 + 2n$ represents the cost in dollars, C, for n painter's caps advertising the walkathon. Which pair of values could represent a number of caps and the cost for that number of caps, (n, C)? Explain your answer.

   (0, 10)   (7, 24)   (15, 30)

11. The equation $d = 3.5t + 50$ represents the distance in meters, d, that a cyclist is from his home after t seconds. Which pair of values represents a point on the graph of this equation? Explain your answer.

   (10, 85)   (0, 0)   (3, 60.5)

12. Ingrid stops at Tara's house on her way to school. Tara's mother says that Tara left 4 minutes ago. Ingrid leaves Tara's house, running to catch up with Tara. The graph below shows the distance each girl is from Tara's house, starting from the time Ingrid leaves Tara's house.

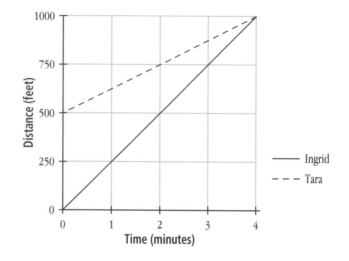

a. In what way is this situation like the race between Henri and Emile? In what way is it different?

b. After how many minutes does Ingrid catch up with Tara?

c. How far from Tara's house does Ingrid catch up with Tara?

d. Each graph intersects the distance axis (the *y*-axis). What information do the points of intersection give about the problem?

e. Which line is steeper? How can you tell from the graph? How is the steepness of each line related to the rate at which the person travels?

f. What do you think the graphs would look like if we extended them to show distance and time after the girls meet?

13. The organizers of the walkathon want to have brochures printed to advertise the event. They get cost estimates from two printing companies. The costs are given by the equations

   Company A: $C = 15 + 0.10n$
   Company B: $C = 0.25n$

where C is the cost in dollars and n is the number of brochures.

   a. Graph both equations on the same set of axes.

   b. For what number of brochures is the cost the same for both companies?

   c. The organizers have $65 to spend on brochures. How many brochures can they have printed if they use company A? If they use company B? Describe the method you used to get your answers.

   d. At what point does each graph intersect the vertical axis? What information does each of these points give?

   e. Explain what the numbers 15 and 0.10 represent in the equation for company A.

   f. Explain what the number 0.25 represents in the equation for company B.

Connections

14. The 1996 Olympic gold medal winner for the 20-kilometer walk was Jefferson Perez from Ecuador. His time was 1 hour, 20 minutes, 7 seconds. Perez's time was not good enough to beat the Olympic record set in 1988 by Josef Pribilinec from Czechoslovakia. Pribilinec's record for the 20-kilometer walk was 1 hour, 19 minutes, 57 seconds. What was the walking rate of each person?

Josef Pribilinec

15. The longest one-day bike race goes from Bordeaux, France, to Paris, France. The record for this race was set in 1981 by Herman van Springel of Belgium. He finished the 363.1-mile race in 13 hours, 35 minutes, 18 seconds. What was Springel's average speed for the race?

16. The longest human-powered sporting event is the Tour de France cycling race. The record average speed for this race is 24.547 miles per hour, which was obtained by Miguel Indurain of Spain in 1992. If the race is 3569 miles long, how long did it take Indurain to complete the race?

17. In 1990, Beate Anders of East Germany set the women's world record for the 3000-meter walk. She completed the race in 11 minutes, 59.36 seconds.

    a. What was Anders' average walking speed?

    b. In 1991, Kerry Ann Saxby of Australia beat Anders' record. She completed the 3000-meter walk in 11 minutes, 51.26 seconds. How much faster did Saxby walk than Anders?

18. **a.** Generate a table and a graph for $y = 5x - 2$. Look back at the graphs you made in this investigation. How is the graph of this equation different from the other graphs you made?

    b. Generate a table and a graph for $y = {}^-2x + 3$. How is the graph different from the other graphs you made in this investigation?

    c. Generate a table and write an equation for the graph below. How is this graph different from the other graphs you made in this investigation?

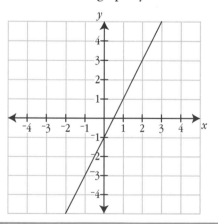

19. The table below shows the amount of orange juice concentrate and water needed to make a given number of batches of juice.

Batches of juice *(b)*	Concentrate *(c)*	Water *(w)*	Juice *(j)*
1	2 cups	3 cups	5 cups
2	4 cups	6 cups	10 cups
3	6 cups	9 cups	15 cups

a. The relationship between the number of batches of juice and the number of cups of concentrate is linear. The equation for this relationship is $c = 2b$. Are there other linear relationships in this table? Make graphs or write equations for the linear relationships you find.

b. A different recipe calls for 3 cups of concentrate and 5 cups of water. Which recipe gives the more "orangey" drink? Explain how you found your answer.

20. The tables below give information about two fruit punch recipes. Each table shows the number of cups of orange juice, pineapple juice, and soda water needed for different quantities of punch. The relationship between cups of orange juice and cups of pineapple juice is linear, and the relationship between cups of orange juice and cups of soda water is linear.

Recipe 1

j	*p*	*s*
1		
2	6	3
3		
4	12	6
5		
6		

Recipe 2

j	*p*	*s*
1		
2		
3	8	6
4		
5		
6	16	12

a. Shannon made recipe 1, using 6 cups of orange juice. How many cups of pineapple juice and how many cups of soda water did she use?

b. Patrick made recipe 2, using 4 cups of orange juice. How many cups of pineapple juice and how many cups of soda water did he use?

Extensions

21. Wind can affect the speed of an airplane. Suppose a plane is making a round-trip from New York City to San Francisco. The plane has a cruising speed of 300 miles per hour. The wind is blowing from west to east at 30 miles per hour. When the plane flies into (in the opposite direction of) the wind, its speed decreases by 30 miles per hour. When the plane flies with (in the same direction as) the wind, its speed increases by 30 miles per hour. The distance between New York City and San Francisco is 3000 miles.

a. Make a table that shows the total time the plane has traveled after each 200-mile interval on its trip from New York City to San Francisco and back.

Distance (miles)	NYC to SF time (hours)	SF to NYC time (hours)
0		
200		
400		
600		
.		
.		
.		

b. On the same set of axes, make graphs of time and distance data for travel in both directions.

c. For each direction, write an equation for the distance, d, traveled in t hours.

d. How long would it take this plane to fly 5000 miles against a 30-mile-per-hour wind? With a 30-mile-per-hour wind? Explain how you found your answers.

22. The table below shows the population of four cities for the past eight years.

Year	Population			
	Deep Valley	Nowhere	Swampville	Mount Silicon
0 (Start)	1000	1000	1000	1000
1	1500	900	1500	2000
2	2000	800	2500	4000
3	2500	750	3000	8000
4	3000	700	5000	16,000
5	3500	725	3000	32,000
6	4000	900	2500	64,000
7	4500	1500	1500	128,000
8	5000	1700	1000	256,000

a. Describe how the population of each city changed over the eight years.

b. Graph the data for each city. Describe how you selected ranges of values for the horizontal and vertical axes.

c. What are the advantages of each representation?

Mathematical Reflections

In this investigation, you learned how to recognize a linear relationship from a table, and you explored the effect that changing the rate has on the table, graph, and equation of a linear relationship. These questions will help you summarize what you have learned:

1. How can you decide whether a relationship is linear by looking at its table or its equation?

2. In the situations you explored, how did the rate—such as the meters per second a student walks or the dollars per mile a sponsor pledges—show up in the table, the graph, and the equation of a linear relationship?

3. How can you compare the rates for two linear relationships by looking at their graphs? Their tables? Their equations?

4. When might you use a graph to answer a question about a linear relationship? When might you use a table? When might you use an equation?

Think about your answers to these questions, discuss your ideas with other students and your teacher, and then write a summary of your findings in your journal.

Exploring Lines with a Graphing Calculator

In the last investigation, you read about the walkathon that Ms. Chang's class is participating in. You considered three possible pledge plans. If A represents the dollars owed and d represents the number of miles walked, we can express these plans with the equations below.

- Leanne's plan: $A = d$
- Gilberto's plan: $A = 2d$
- Alana's plan: $A = 5 + 0.5d$

In this investigation, you will learn how to use a graphing calculator to help you answer questions like these:

What does Leanne's equation mean?

Using Gilberto's plan, how much will a sponsor owe a student who walks 5 miles?

Using Alana's plan, how far will a student have to walk to earn $17 from each sponsor?

Did you know?

Have you ever seen a walking race? You may have thought the walking style of the racers seemed rather strange. Race walkers must follow two rules:

1. The walker must always have one foot in contact with the ground.

2. The walker's leg must be straight from the time it strikes the ground until it passes under the body.

A champion race walker can cover a mile in about 6.5 minutes. It takes most people 15 to 20 minutes to walk a mile.

Getting to the Point

To work on this problem, you will need the tables and graphs you made in Problem 2.3.

Problem 3.1

Look at the table and the graph you made for Alana's pledge plan.

A. The point (14, 12) is on the graph of Alana's plan. Write a question you could answer by locating this point.

B. How can you use the equation for Alana's plan to check the answer to the question you wrote in part A?

C. 1. For a sponsor to owe a student $17 under Alana's pledge plan, how many miles would the student have to walk?

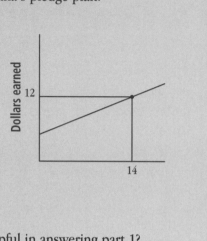

    2. Was the graph or the equation more helpful in answering part 1?

■ **Problem 3.1 Follow-Up**

1. Aretha is trying to answer a question about Alana's pledge plan. She writes $A = 5 + 0.5(28)$. What question is she trying to answer?

2. a. Daniel is trying to answer a question about Alana's pledge plan. He writes $46 = 5 + 0.5d$. What question is he trying to answer?

    b. Daniel decides to use a calculator to help him answer the question from part a. He enters Alana's equation as $Y_1 = 5 + 0.5X$ and presses ⬚GRAPH⬚. He uses the ⬚TRACE⬚ key to search for an answer. Help Daniel interpret the information in the window below to determine an answer to his question.

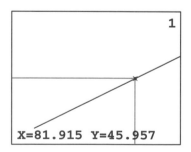

    c. Daniel could have answered the question by making a table. Use your calculator to make a table for $Y_1 = 5 + 0.5X$. Copy a section of the table you could use to answer Daniel's question.

3.2 Graphing Lines

A graphing calculator can be helpful for answering questions like those in Problem 3.1 and Problem 3.1 Follow-Up. When you use a graphing calculator, you need to make decisions about the range of values and the scale interval for each axis. These values are called *window settings* because they determine what part of the graph will be displayed in the calculator's window.

Below are two examples of window settings and the corresponding graph windows. For each example, try to make sense of what the ranges and the scale intervals are for the *x*- and *y*-axes.

Window 1

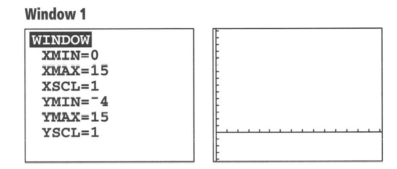

Window 2

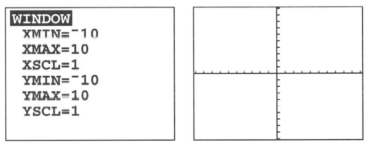

The settings for window 1 use a different range for each axis. The range of *x* values is from 0 to 15, which is a spread of 15 units. The range of *y* values is from ⁻4 to 15, which is a spread of 19 units. The scale interval for both axes is 1, which means that each tick mark represents 1 unit.

Window 2 is the *standard window* on many graphing calculators. These are the settings the calculator uses unless you change them. In this window, both axes have a range from ⁻10 to 10 and a scale interval of 1.

Notice that, in each window, the length of 1 unit (the distance between tick marks) is different on the *x*-axis than it is on the *y*-axis. Can you explain why?

Think about this!

How far would a student have to walk to raise $8.50 from each sponsor under Alana's plan?

Ali and Tamara are using graphing calculators to answer this question. They both enter the equation $Y_1 = 5 + 0.5X$. Ali uses window 1 for his graph, and Tamara uses window 2. Both students use TRACE to find the solution.

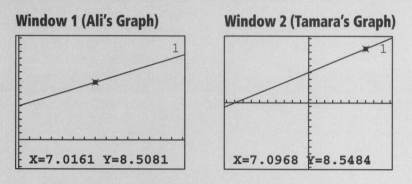

Window 1 (Ali's Graph)

X=7.0161 Y=8.5081

Window 2 (Tamara's Graph)

X=7.0968 Y=8.5484

- What does the X value displayed at the bottom of each window mean? What does the Y value mean?

- How could you interpret the information displayed in the windows to answer the question above? How could you check your answer?

You have explored pledge plans suggested by Leanne, Gilberto, and Alana. In this problem, you will explore some plans suggested by other students.

Problem 3.2

In A–D, consider the following suggested pledge plans. In each equation, y is the amount owed in dollars, and x is the number of miles walked.

i. $y = 3x$ **ii.** $y = {}^-2x$ **iii.** $y = 5x - 3$

iv. $y = {}^-x + 6$ **v.** $y = 2$

A. What does each pledge plan mean?

B. Without using your graphing calculator, make a table of x and y values for each pledge plan. Use the x values 1, 2, 3, 4, and 5. Use your tables to help you decide which plans are reasonable. Explain how you made your decisions.

C. Graph each pledge plan with a graphing calculator. Use a window that shows the graph clearly. Make a sketch of the graph you see.

D. For each pledge plan, tell whether the y values increase, decrease, or stay the same as the x values increase. How can you tell from the graph? From the table? From the equation?

■ Problem 3.2 Follow-Up

1. For each of the five pledge plans, give the coordinates of the points where the line crosses the x- and y-axes. (Check that the coordinates you give fit the equation. Sometimes the decimal values your calculator gives are only approximations.)
2. Ali says that $x = {}^-1$ makes the equation $^-8 = {}^-3 + 5x$ true. Tamara tries this value in the equation. She says Ali is wrong because $^-3 + 5(^-1)$ is $^-2$, not $^-8$. Why do you think these students found different answers?

3.3 Finding Solutions

In this problem, you will explore the relationship between a general equation, such as $y = 5 + 0.5x$, and the equation you get by substituting a value for either x or y, such as $8 = 5 + 0.5x$ or $y = 5 + 0.5(3)$. You will continue to work with the pledge plan equations from Problem 3.2.

By now you've probably noticed that values for x and y come in pairs. In the pledge equations, if you know the distance walked, x, you can find the amount a sponsor owes, y. If you know the amount a sponsor owes, y, you can find the distance walked, x. You can express related x and y values as **coordinate pairs** in the form (x, y). For example, the pairs (6, 8) and (3, 6.5) fit Alana's equation. Can you explain what each pair means?

Problem 3.3

In A–D, consider the following equations.

i. $y = 3x$ **ii.** $y = {}^-2x$ **iii.** $y = 5x - 3$
iv. $y = {}^-x + 6$ **v.** $y = 2$

A. 1. Which equation has a graph you can trace to find the value of x that makes $^-8 = 5x - 3$ a true statement?

     2. Use your graphing calculator to find the value of x. We call this value the *solution* to the equation $^-8 = 5x - 3$.

B. 1. Which equation has a table you can use to find the value of x that makes $6.8 = {}^-2x$ a true statement?

     2. Make a table with your graphing calculator, and find the value of x. Copy the part of the table you used to find the solution.

C. Find solutions for the equations $^-8 = 5x - 3$ and $6.8 = {}^-2x$ by reasoning about what the equations mean rather than by using graphs or tables. Explain how you found the solutions.

D. 1. How does finding the solution to $^-8 = 5x - 3$ help you find a coordinate pair that fits the equation $y = 5x - 3$?

     2. Find three other coordinate pairs that fit the equation $y = 5x - 3$. How can you prove your coordinate pairs fit the equation?

■ Problem 3.3 Follow-Up

1. Are the points for the coordinate pairs you found for $y = 5x - 3$ on the graph of $y = 5x - 3$? Explain your answer.

2. In part B of Problem 3.3, you found the solution to the equation $6.8 = {}^-2x$. Based on the solution, what coordinate pair do you know must fit the equation $y = {}^-2x$? How is this coordinate pair related to the graph of $y = {}^-2x$?

3. a. By substituting values for y, write three equations that are related to the equation $y = {}^-3x + 6$.

     b. Solve each of your equations from part a. Explain how you found each solution.

     c. Use the solutions from part b to find the coordinates of three points on the graph of $y = {}^-3x + 6$.

     d. Use your graphing calculator to check your answers to part c. Explain how you know your answers are correct.

Planning a Skating Party

You have studied lots of linear equations. Here are some examples:

$y = x$ $y = 2x$ $y = 5 + 0.5x$ $y = 45 + x$ $y = {}^-3x + 6$

All the linear equations you have studied can be written in the form $y = mx + b$. For the equation $y = x$, m is 1 and b is 0. For $y = 2x$, m is 2 and b is 0. For $y = 5 + 0.5x$, m is 0.5 and b is 5. What are the values of m and b for $y = 45 + x$ and $y = {}^-3x + 6$?

When we substitute 0 for x in $y = mx + b$, we get $y = b$. This means that the point $(0, b)$ lies on the line. The point $(0, b)$ is called the **y-intercept.** It is the point where the line crosses the y-axis. To save time, we sometimes refer to the number b, rather than the point $(0, b)$, as the y-intercept. You found y-intercepts for some equations in Problem 3.2 Follow-Up

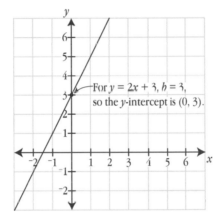

For $y = 2x + 3$, $b = 3$, so the y-intercept is $(0, 3)$.

If the b in $y = mx + b$ is 0 (in other words, if the equation is of the form $y = mx$) then the y-intercept is $(0, 0)$, or the **origin.** For example, the graphs of Leanne's pledge plan $y = x$ and Gilberto's pledge plan $y = 2x$ both pass through the origin.

The m in $y = mx + b$ is called the **coefficient** of x. In Investigation 2, you found that the value of m indicates the steepness of the line. For example, when you graphed equations for students' walking rates, you found that the graph of $y = 2x$ was steeper than the graph of $y = x$ but less steep than the graph of $y = 2.5x$. You also discovered that the sign of m—that is, whether m is positive or negative—determines whether a line slants upward or downward.

In the last problem, you used a graphing calculator to find specific points on the graphs of linear equations. In this problem, you will use a graphing calculator to find the point where two graphs cross. This point is called the **point of intersection** of the graphs.

Problem 3.4

Suppose your class is planning a skating party to celebrate the end of the school year. Your committee is in charge of finding a place to rent in-line skates for a reasonable price. You get quotes from two companies:

Roll-Away Skates charges $5 per person.
Wheelie's Skates and Stuff charges $100 plus $3 per person.

Which company should you choose if you want to keep the cost to a minimum? Explain how you made your choice.

■ Problem 3.4 Follow-Up

In these problems, let y be the total cost to rent the skates and x be the number of people attending the party.

1. a. For each company, write an equation for the relationship between the number of people and the cost.

   b. In the same window, graph the equations for both companies.

   c. What range of values did you use for the number of people? For the rental cost? How did you select these ranges?

2. a. On which graph is the point (8, 40)? What does this point mean in terms of the cost to rent skates?

   b. On which graph is the point (8, 124)? What does this point mean in terms of the cost to rent skates?

   c. Find the point of intersection of the two graphs. What does this point mean in terms of the cost to rent skates?

3. If you write a linear equation in the form $y = mx + b$, the y-intercept is $(0, b)$.

    a. Find the y-intercepts for the equations you graphed in question 1.

    b. What do the y-intercepts mean in terms of the cost to rent skates?

    c. How do the y-intercepts appear on the graphs?

    d. Display the table for the equations. How do the y-intercepts appear in the table?

4. What are the coefficients of x in the equations you graphed in question 1? What do these coefficients mean in terms of the cost to rent skates? What effect do the coefficients have on the graphs?

5. Which company would you choose if 100 students are planning to attend the party? Why?

6. If your budget for skate rental is $250, how many pairs of skates can you rent from each company?

As you work on these ACE questions, use your calculator whenever you need it.

Applications

In 1–4, do parts a–e.

1. $y = 1.5x$ **2.** $y = {}^-3x + 10$ **3.** $y = {}^-2x + 6$ **4.** $y = 2x + 5$

    a.   Graph the equation on your calculator, and make a sketch of the line you see.

    b.   Give the ranges of values you used for the x- and y-axes.

    c.   Do the y values increase, decrease, or stay the same as the x values increase?

    d.   Give the y-intercept.

    e.   List the coordinates of three points on the line.

5.   The school band decides to sell chocolate bars to raise money for an upcoming trip. The cost and the revenue (total sales, or income) of selling the candy bars are represented on the graph below.

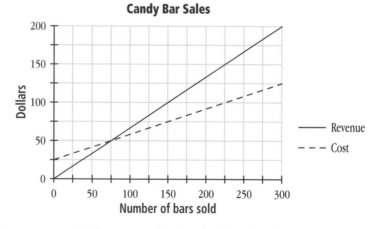

    a.   How many candy bars must the band sell to break even?

    b.   What would be the revenue from selling 50 candy bars? 125 candy bars?

    c.   How many candy bars must the band sell for the revenue to be $200? How much of this revenue would be profit?

6. a. At the left below, the graphs from question 5 are shown in a calculator's graph window. The window settings are shown at the right. Copy the graph window, and use the window settings to label the axes to show where the scale values 50, 100, 150, and so on are located.

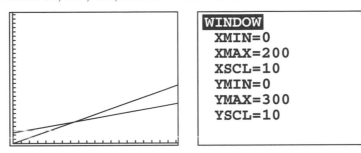

```
WINDOW
  XMIN=0
  XMAX=200
  XSCL=10
  YMIN=0
  YMAX=300
  YSCL=10
```

b. Below are the same two graphs shown in a different graph window. Copy the graph window, and use the window settings to label the tick marks.

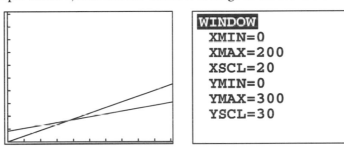

```
WINDOW
  XMIN=0
  XMAX=200
  XSCL=20
  YMIN=0
  YMAX=300
  YSCL=30
```

7. In a–c, use the equation $y = 2x + 10$.

a. By making a graph on your calculator, find the value of y when $x = 15$.

b. By making a graph on your calculator, find the value of x when $y = 35$.

c. Make a sketch of the graph of $y = 2x + 10$, and label the points that represent the pairs of values you found in parts a and b.

8. In a–c, use the equation $y = {}^-3.5x - 9$.

a. By making a graph on your calculator, find the value of y when $x = 5$.

b. By making a graph on your calculator, find the value of x when $y = {}^-40$.

c. Make a sketch of the graph of $y = {}^-3.5x - 9$, and label the points that represent the pairs of values you found in parts a and b.

In 9–12, do parts a–c.

9. $y = 5x + 24$ and $y = {}^-3x - 8$

10. $y = {}^-2.5x + 15$ and $y = x - 10$

11. $y = x + 10$ and $y = 8 - 2x$

12. $y = 6$ and $y = 4 + 2x$

a. With your graphing calculator, graph both equations in the same window. Use window settings that allow you to see the point where the two graphs intersect. What ranges of x and y values did you use for your window?

b. Find the point of intersection for the graphs.

c. Test the point of intersection you found by substituting its coordinates into the equations. Do the coordinates fit the equations exactly? Explain why or why not.

13. In Problem 2.4, Emile gave Henri a head start of 45 meters. Now suppose Emile does not give his brother a head start.

a. Write a new equation for the distance Henri is from the starting line after a given number of seconds. Describe the graph of this new equation.

b. How do this new graph and equation compare with the original graph and equation?

c. What effect did Henri's head start have on the original graph? On the original equation?

14. For Valentine's Day, students at Holmes Middle School will sell roses to raise money for a school party. The students can buy the roses from a wholesaler for 50¢ each. In addition to buying the roses, they need to spend $60 for ribbon and paper to wrap the flowers and for materials to advertise the sale. They will sell each flower for $1.30. They will take orders in advance so that they know how many roses they will need.

a. How many roses must the students sell to break even?

b. How much profit will the students earn if they sell 50 roses? 100 roses? 200 roses?

15. A new movie theater opened in Lani's neighborhood. The theater offers a yearly membership for which customers pay a fee of $50, after which they pay only $1 per movie. Nonmembers pay $4.50 per movie. Lani is trying to figure out whether to buy a membership. She writes these cost equations.

$$C_M = 50 + n \qquad \text{and} \qquad C_N = 4.5n$$

where n is the number of movies seen in one year, C_M is the yearly cost in dollars for a member, and C_N is the yearly cost in dollars for a nonmember.

a. If Lani sees ten movies this year, what would be her cost under each plan?

b. How many movies must Lani see this year to make the yearly membership a better deal?

c. What does the y-intercept in each equation tell you about this situation?

d. What does the coefficient of n in each equation tell you about this situation?

In 16 and 17, use the following information: You are on the committee to select a DJ for a school party. The committee has obtained price quotes from three DJs:

Tom's Tunes charges $60 an hour.
Solidus' Sounds charges $100 plus $40 an hour.
Light Plastic charges $175 plus $30 an hour.

16. **a.** Which DJ would you choose? What variables might affect your decision?

b. For each DJ, write an equation you could use to calculate the total cost from the number of hours worked. Let y be the total cost and x be the number of hours worked.

c. Graph all three equations in the same window of your calculator. Make a sketch of the graphs you see.

d. What information does the coefficient of x represent in each equation?

e. What information does the y-intercept represent in each equation?

17. Use your calculator to answer a–c.

  a. For what number of hours are the costs for Tom's Tunes and Solidus' Sounds equal? What is the cost for that time?

  b. What would be the cost for each DJ if he or she worked $8\frac{1}{2}$ hours?

  c. You have $450 to spend on a DJ. How many hours could each DJ work for this price?

Connections

In 18–21, tell what values of x make y negative.

18. $y = {}^-2x - 5$ **19.** $y = {}^-5$ **20.** $y = 2x - 5$ **21.** $y = \frac{3}{2}x - \frac{1}{4}$

22. In a–c, explain how you could use the display shown to find the solution to $22 = 100 - 3x$.

  a.

X	Y₁
21	37
22	34
23	31
24	28
25	25
26	22

Y₁ ▤ 100 - 3X

  b.

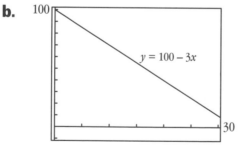

c.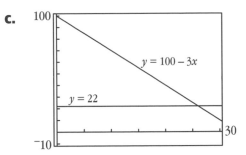

23. In a and b, explain how you could use the display shown to find the solution to $100 - 3x = 2x - 50$.

a.

X	Y₁	Y₂
25	25	0
26	22	2
27	19	4
28	16	6
29	13	8
30	10	10

Y₂⊟2X−50

b.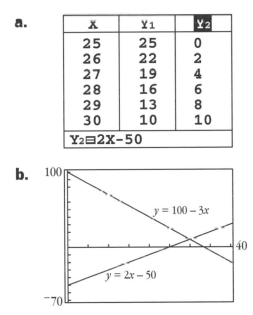

In 24–26, tell whether or not the equation represents a linear relationship, and explain your answer.

24. $y = 2x$ **25.** $y = \frac{2}{x}$ **26.** $y = x^2$

Extensions

27. **a.** On grid paper, graph each pair of lines below on the same set of axes. Use the same scale for the *x*- and *y*-axes for each pair. When you are finished, look at the graphs for all four pairs of equations. What patterns do you observe? Use what you know about the influence of *m* and *b* on the graph of $y = mx + b$ to explain why these patterns might occur.

    i. $y = 1.2x + 3$ and $y = 1.2x$ **ii.** $y = 4$ and $y = {}^-2$

    iii. $y = x - 19$ and $y = 4 + x$ **iv.** $y = {}^-3.6x$ and $y = 5 - 3.6x$

b. On grid paper, graph each pair of lines below on the same set of axes. Use the same scale for the *x*- and *y*-axes. When you are finished, look at the graphs for all four pairs of equations. What patterns do you observe? Compare the coefficients of *x* in each pair, and describe any relationships you see.

    i. $y = 2x + 1$ and $y = -\frac{1}{2}x - 2$ **ii.** $y = x - 3$ and $y = {}^-x$

    iii. $y = x$ and $y = {}^-x$ **iv.** $y = \frac{5}{4}x$ and $y = -\frac{4}{5}x + 4$

c. Graph the equations from part b on your graphing calculator, using the same scales you used in your hand-drawn graphs. Explain any differences you see between the hand-drawn graphs and the calculator graphs.

d. Use your observations from parts a and b to predict the relationship between the graphs of the pairs of equations below. Check your predictions by graphing the equations.

    i. $y = 4x$ and $y = -\frac{1}{4}x$ **ii.** $y = x + 2$ and $y = {}^-x + 5$

    iii. $y = 0.5x + 2$ and $y = 0.5x - 2$ **iv.** $y = 2x + 1$ and $y = 2x$

28. For a given latitude and longitude, the temperature decreases as the altitude increases. The formula for calculating the temperature, T, at a given altitude is

$$T = t - \frac{d}{150}$$

where t is the ground temperature in degrees Celsius and d is the altitude in meters.

a. If the ground temperature is $0°C$, what is the temperature at an altitude of 1500 meters?

b. If the temperature at an altitude of 300 meters is $26°C$, what is the ground temperature?

29. a. Which one of the following points is on the line $y = 3x - 7$?

$(3, 3)$ $\qquad$ $(3, 2)$ $\qquad$ $(3, 1)$ $\qquad$ $(3, 0)$

Describe where each of the other three points is in relationship to the line.

b. Find another point on the line $y = 3x - 7$ and three more points above the line.

c. The equation $y = 3x - 7$ is true for $(4, 5)$ and $(7, 14)$. Find two points for which the inequality $y < 3x - 7$ is true and two points for which the inequality $y > 3x - 7$ is true.

Mathematical Reflections

In this investigation, you learned how to use tables and graphs to solve problems about linear relationships, and you discovered how a point in a table or on a graph relates to the corresponding equation. You also learned how to find the *y*-intercept of a relationship from a table, graph, or equation. These questions will help you summarize what you have learned:

1. What are some of the advantages and disadvantages of using a graphing calculator to answer questions about linear situations?

2. Explain how to find the *y*-intercept of a linear relationship from a table, from a graph, and from an equation.

3. In Investigation 2, you explored the effect that the rate has on the graph of a linear relationship. In this investigation, you looked at the meaning of particular points on the graph, including the *y*-intercept. Summarize what you know about the graph of a linear equation of the form $y = mx + b$.

4. To check whether a given point fits a linear relationship, you can make a table, trace a graph, or substitute the coordinates into an equation. When you substitute values into an equation, you need to be careful about the order in which you do the calculations. Check whether the point ($^-2$, 13) is on the line $y = 5 - 4x$ by substituting the coordinates into the equation. Show and explain each step you take so that it is easy to see the order in which you did your calculations.

   Think about your answers to these questions, discuss your ideas with other students and your teacher, and then write a summary of your findings in your journal.

Solving Equations

In previous investigations, you answered questions about linear relationships by using graphs and tables and by reasoning about the numbers involved. In this investigation, you will learn how to answer such questions by writing and solving linear equations.

4.1 Paying in Installments

The Unlimited Store allows any customer who buys merchandise costing over $30 to pay on an installment plan. The customer pays $30 down and then pays $15 a month until the item is paid for.

Problem 4.1

Suppose you buy a $195 CD-ROM drive from the Unlimited Store on an installment plan. How many months will it take you to pay for the drive? Describe how you found your answer.

■ Problem 4.1 Follow-Up

1. Write down the sequence of steps you used to find the solution to Problem 4.1. Try to use mathematical symbols and not just words to describe your steps.

2. Make up a problem similar to Problem 4.1, and solve it using your method from question 1.

Using the Symbolic Method

The students in your class may have found several ways to solve Problem 4.1. Some may have used a table or a graph. Others may have found a way to reason about the quantities in the problem. For example, in Ms. Winslow's class, one student reasoned as follows:

"If I pay $30 down, I will have $195 − $30, or $165, left to pay. If I pay $15 a month, then it will take me $165 ÷ 15 = 11, months to pay for the drive."

You can also solve Problem 4.1 by writing and solving an equation. To write an equation, you could reason as follows:

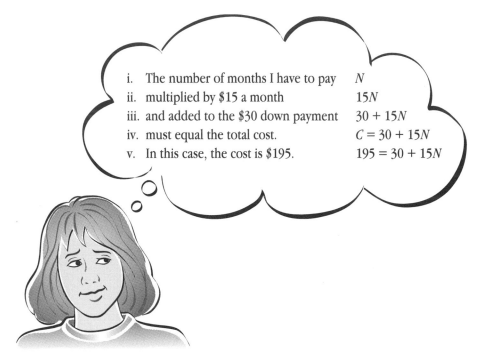

i.	The number of months I have to pay	N
ii.	multiplied by $15 a month	$15N$
iii.	and added to the $30 down payment	$30 + 15N$
iv.	must equal the total cost.	$C = 30 + 15N$
v.	In this case, the cost is $195.	$195 = 30 + 15N$

To find the number of months you must pay, you need to find the value of N that makes the equation $195 = 30 + 15N$ a true statement. This is called *solving the equation* for the variable N.

From your work in the last investigation, you know you can solve $195 = 30 + 15N$ by making a table or a graph of the general equation $C = 30 + 15N$. Now you will learn to solve $195 = 30 + 15N$ by *operating on the symbols* in the equation.

Thinking	Manipulating the Symbols
	$195 = 30 + 15N$
"I want to buy a CD-ROM drive that costs \$195. To pay for the drive on the installment plan, I must pay \$30 down and \$15 a month."	$195 = 30 + 15N$
"After I pay the \$30 down payment, I can subtract this from the cost. To keep the sides of the equation equal, I must subtract 30 from both sides."	$195 - 30 = 30 - 30 + 15N$
"I now owe \$165, which I will pay in monthly installments of \$15."	$165 = 15N$
"I need to separate \$165 into payments of \$15. This means I need to divide it by 15. To keep the sides of the equation equal, I must divide both sides by 15."	$\dfrac{165}{15} = \dfrac{15N}{15}$
"There are 11 groups of \$15 in \$165, so it will take 11 months."	$11 = N$

After you solve an equation, you should always check your solution by substituting it back into the original equation. Here are the steps you would follow to check the solution to the equation above.

$$195 = 30 + 15N$$
$$195 = 30 + 15(11)$$
$$195 = 30 + 165$$
$$195 = 195$$

Review the table above. The strategy we used to solve the equation was to *undo,* or *reverse,* the operations until the variable was alone on one side of the equation. Notice that we applied each reverse operation to *both* sides of the equation. We will refer to this strategy for solving an equation as the *symbolic method.*

Problem 4.2

Karen wants to buy a stove from the Unlimited Store on an installment plan. The stove costs $305.

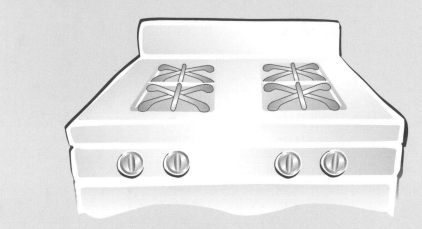

A. Write an equation you could solve to find the number of months it will take Karen to pay for the stove.

B. Solve your equation by using the symbolic method. How many months will it take Karen to pay for the stove?

■ Problem 4.2 Follow-Up

1. In a–d, use the symbolic method to solve the equation for x. Check your answers.
   a. $y = 2.5x$ when $y = 175$
   b. $y = 19 + 3x$ when $y = 64$
   c. $y = 2x - 50$ when $y = 15$
   d. $y = {}^-2x + 14$ when $y = 60$

2. What other methods could you use to solve for x in the equations in question 1?

4.3 Analyzing Bones

Forensic scientists can estimate a person's height by measuring the length of certain bones, including the femur, the tibia, the humerus, and the radius.

The table below gives equations for the relationships between the length of each bone and the height for males and females. These relationships were found by scientists after much study and data collection. In the table, F represents the length of the femur, T the length of the tibia, H the length of the humerus, R the length of the radius, and h the person's height. All measurements are in centimeters.

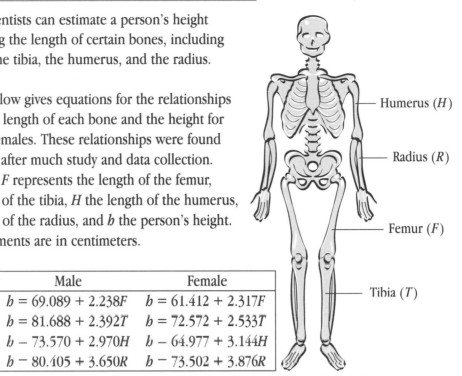

Humerus (H)

Radius (R)

Femur (F)

Tibia (T)

Bone	Male	Female
Femur	$h = 69.089 + 2.238F$	$h = 61.412 + 2.317F$
Tibia	$h = 81.688 + 2.392T$	$h = 72.572 + 2.533T$
Humerus	$h = 73.570 + 2.970H$	$h = 64.977 + 3.144H$
Radius	$h = 80.405 + 3.650R$	$h = 73.502 + 3.876R$

Source: George Knill. "Mathematics in Forensic Science." *Mathematics Teacher* (February 1981): 31–32.

Problem 4.3

Use the equations on page 57 to answer parts A–D.

A. How tall is a female if her femur is 46.2 centimeters long?

B. How tall is a male if his tibia is 50.1 centimeters long?

C. If a woman is 152 centimeters (about 5 feet) tall, how long is her femur? Her tibia? Her humerus? Her radius?

D. If a man is 183 centimeters (about 6 feet) tall, how long is his femur? His tibia? His humerus? His radius?

■ Problem 4.3 Follow-Up

For one of the bones discussed above, graph the equations for males and females on the same set of axes. What do the *x*- and *y*-intercepts represent in terms of this problem? Does this make sense? Why?

As you work on these ACE questions, use your calculator whenever you need it.

Applications

1. Find x if $326 = 4x$.

2. Find p if $93 = 16 - 5p$.

3. Find n if $321.5 = 16n - 25.5$.

In 4–6, do parts a and b by using the symbolic method and by using a graphing calculator.

4. $y = x - 15$
   a. Find y if $x = 9.4$.   **b.** Find x if $y = 29$.

5. $y = 10 - 2.5x$
   a. Find y if $x = 3.2$.   **b.** Find x if $y = 85$.

6. $y = 5x - 15$
   a. Find y if $x = 1$.   **b.** Find x if $y = 50$.

7. In questions 4–6, you solved linear equations by using the symbolic method and by using a graphing calculator. Compare these two methods. Which do you prefer? Why?

8. Below is a student's solution to the equation $58.5 = 3.5x - 6$. The student made an error. Find the error, and give the correct solution.

$$58.5 = 3.5x - 6$$
$$58.5 - 6 = 3.5x$$
$$52.5 = 3.5x$$
$$\frac{52.5}{3.5} = x$$
$$\text{so } 15 = x$$

9. The number of times a cricket chirps in a minute is a function of the temperature. You can use the formula

$$n = 4t - 160$$

to determine the number of chirps, n, a cricket makes in a minute when the temperature is t degrees Fahrenheit. If you want to estimate the temperature by counting cricket chirps, it is easier to use the following form of the equation:

$$t = \tfrac{1}{4}n + 40$$

a. At 60°F, how many times does a cricket chirp in a minute?

b. What is the temperature if a cricket chirps 150 times in a minute?

c. At what temperature does a cricket stop chirping?

d. Sketch a graph of the equation with number of chirps on the x-axis and temperature on the y-axis. What information does the y-intercept give you?

10. At Fabulous Fabian's Bakery, the cost, C, and revenue, R, to make and sell N cakes per month are given by the equations below.

$$C = 800 + 3.20N \qquad \text{and} \qquad R = 8.50N$$

a. Fabian sold 100 cakes in January. What were his cost and his revenue? Did he make a profit?

b. In April, Fabian's revenue was $1105. How many cakes did he sell?

c. What was the cost of producing the number of cakes from part b?

d. What is the break-even point between cost and revenue?

e. In each equation, what information do the y-intercept and the coefficient of N give you?

11. In a and b, find the mystery number, and explain your reasoning.

   a. If you add 15 to 3 times this mystery number, you get 78. What is the mystery number?

   b. If you subtract 27 from 5 times this mystery number, you get 83. What is the mystery number?

   c. Make up clues for a riddle whose answer is 9.

Connections

12. When a person reaches the age of 30, his or her height starts decreasing by approximately 0.06 centimeter per year.

   a. If a basketball player is 6 feet, 6 inches tall on his thirtieth birthday, about how tall will he be at age 80? (Remember, 1 inch ≈ 2.5 centimeters.)

   b. Myron's 80-year-old grandmother is 160 centimeters tall. About how tall was she at age 30?

13. World Connections long-distance phone company charges $50 a month plus 10¢ a minute for each call.

   a. Write an equation for the total monthly cost, C, for m minutes of long-distance calls.

   b. A customer made $10\frac{1}{2}$ hours of long-distance calls in a month. How much was his bill for that month?

   c. A customer received a $75 long-distance bill for last month's calls. How many minutes of long-distance calls did she make?

   d. The International Links long-distance phone company has no monthly fee and charges 18¢ a minute for long-distance calls. Compare the World Connections long-distance plan to the International Links plan. Under what circumstances is it cheaper to use International Links?

14. Give the formulas for finding the circumference and the area of a circle if you know its radius. Tell whether each equation represents a linear relationship.

15. **a.** Write an equation for the distance covered by a car traveling 50 miles per hour for a given number of hours.

    b. Write an equation for the time it takes to go 20 miles at a given rate of speed.

    c. Is either of the equations in parts a and b linear?

Extensions

16. The Small World long-distance phone company charges 55¢ for the first minute of a long-distance call and 23¢ for each additional minute.

    a. How much would a 10-minute long-distance call cost?

    b. If a call costs $4.55, how long did the call last?

    c. Write an equation for the total cost, C, of an m-minute long-distance call.

17. The maximum weight allowed in an elevator is 1500 pounds.

    a. If ten children are in the elevator, how many adults can get in? Assume the average weight per adult is 150 pounds and the average weight per child is 40 pounds.

    b. If six adults are in the elevator, how many children can get in?

    c. Write an equation for the number of adults, A, and the number of children, C, the elevator can hold.

Mathematical Reflections

In this investigation, you learned how to solve equations by operating on the symbols. These questions will help you summarize what you have learned:

1 Describe the symbolic method for solving an equation of the form $y = mx + b$ for the variable x when you know the value of y. Use an example to illustrate the method.

2 Describe how you would use a graphing calculator to solve a linear equation of the form $y = mx + b$ for the variable x when you know the value of y. Use an example to illustrate the process.

Think about your answers to these questions, discuss your ideas with other students and your teacher, and then write a summary of your findings in your journal.

Exploring Slope

All the linear situations you have explored in this unit involve rates. For example, you worked with walking rates expressed as meters per second and pledge rates expressed as dollars per mile. In these situations, you found that the rate affects the following things:

- the steepness of the graph
- the coefficient, *m*, of *x* in the equation $y = mx + b$
- the amount the *y* values in the table change for each unit change in the *x* values

All of these things are related to the *slope* of the line. In this investigation, you will learn what the slope of a line is, and you will discover how you can determine the slope from the graph, equation, or table of values for a linear relationship.

5.1 Climbing Stairs

Climbing stairs is good exercise. Some athletes run up and down stairs as part of their training. The steepness of stairs determines how difficult they are to climb. Stairs that are very steep are more difficult to climb than stairs that rise gradually. Examining the steepness of stairs can help you understand the idea of steepness, or slope, of a line.

Think about this!

Consider the following questions about the stairs you encounter at home, in your school, and in other buildings:

- How can you describe the steepness of the stairs?
- Is the steepness the same between any two consecutive steps for a particular set of stairs?

The steepness of stairs is determined by the ratio of the **rise** to the **run** for each step. The rise and run are labeled in the diagram below.

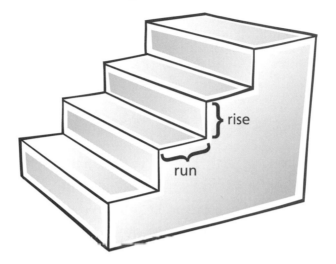

Carpenters have developed guidelines to ensure the stairs they build are relatively easy for a person to climb. In some states, carpenters work with these guidelines:

- The ratio of rise to run for each step should be between 0.45 and 0.60.
- The rise plus the run for each step should be between 17 and 17.5 inches.

Problem 5.1

Determine the steepness of a set of stairs.

To calculate the steepness you will need to measure the rise and the run of a step. Measure at least two steps in the set of stairs you choose. Make a sketch of the stairs, and label it with the measurements you found.

How do the stairs you measured compare with the guidelines above?

1. Make and label a scale drawing of stairs that don't meet the carpenters' guidelines. Explain why the stairs you drew are steeper (or less steep) than the stairs described in the guidelines.

2. You can use the ideas about the steepness of stairs to find the steepness of a ramp.

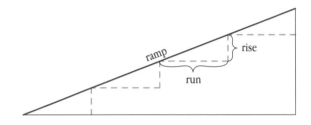

In one state, the construction code for an access ramp is a rise of 1 foot for a run of 12 feet. The access ramp at a football stadium in this state has a rise of 1 foot for a run of 8 feet. Many people in wheelchairs cannot get their chairs up the ramp without help. Make scale drawings of the stadium ramp and a ramp meeting the state code.

5.2 Finding the Slope of a Line

The method for finding the steepness of stairs suggests a way to find the steepness of a line. A line drawn from the bottom step to the top step of a set of stairs will touch each step in one point. The rise and the run of a step are the vertical and the horizontal changes, respectively, between two points on the line.

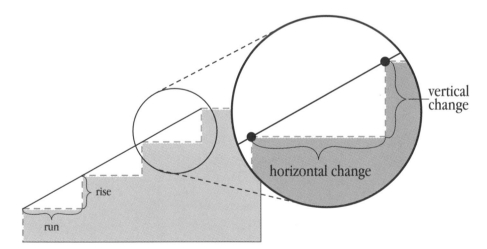

If you choose two points on a line, you can draw a "step" from one point to the other.

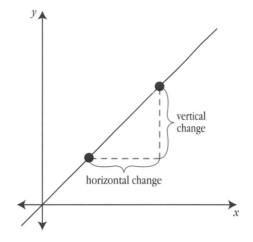

The steepness of the line is the ratio of rise to run, or vertical change to horizontal change, for this step. We call the steepness of a line its **slope.**

$$\text{slope} = \frac{\text{vertical change}}{\text{horizontal change}}$$

Unlike the steepness of stairs, the slope of a line can be negative. To determine the slope of a line, you need to consider the direction, or sign, of the vertical and horizontal change from one point to another. If one of these changes is negative, the slope will be negative. Lines that slant *upward* from left to right have *positive slope;* lines that slant *downward* from left to right have *negative slope.*

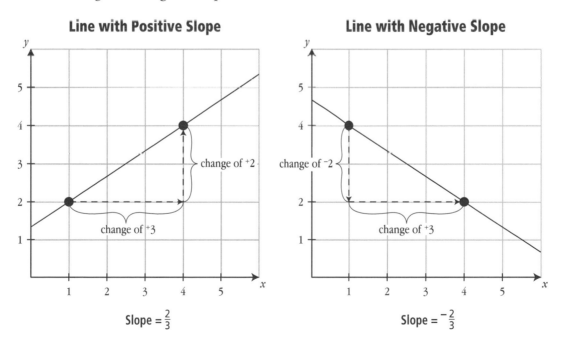

Do parts A–D for each equation below.

i. $y = 2x$ **ii.** $y = {}^-3x$ **iii.** $y = 5 + 2x$
iv. $y = \frac{1}{2}x + 2$ **v.** $y = 2 - 3x$

A. Make a table of x and y values for the equation. Use the x values ${}^-3, {}^-2, {}^-1, 0,$ 1, 2, 3, and 4.

B. On grid paper, make a graph of the equation.

C. Choose two points on the line, and compute the ratio of the vertical change to the horizontal change from one point to the other. Would you get the same ratio if you had chosen two different points? Choose two different points, and check your answer.

D. The ratio you computed in part C is the slope of the line. How is the slope of the line related to the table of values for the line? How is it related to the equation for the line?

■ **Problem 5.2 Follow-Up**

Use the ideas you have learned about slope and about vertical and horizontal change to explain why the line for $y = 3x$ is steeper than the line for $y = x$.

5.3 Connecting Points

For any two points, there is exactly one straight line that can be drawn through both points. In this problem, you will be given the coordinates of two points. Your task will be to find information about the line through these points—including its slope, its y-intercept, and the coordinates of other points that lie on the line.

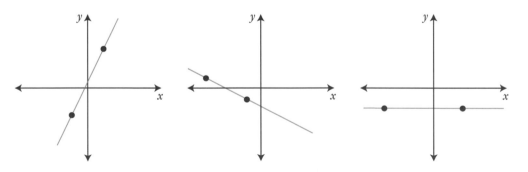

Problem 5.3

Do parts A–E for each pair of points below.

i. (2, 6) and (0, 4)   ii. (2, 3) and (4, 6)   iii. (0, 3) and (1, 4)

iv. (⁻1, 3) and (1, 0)   v. (1, 4) and (3, 4)   vi. (4, 1) and (⁻4, 2)

A. Plot the points on a coordinate grid, and draw the line that passes through them.

B. Do the y values for points on the line increase, decrease, or stay the same as the x values increase?

C. Find the slope of the line.

D. Mark and label at least three other points on the line, and record the x and y values for the points in an organized table. Does the pattern in your table confirm the slope you found in part B?

E. Use the graph or the table to find the y-intercept of the line.

Problem 5.3 Follow-Up

1. How can you use the slope of a line to determine whether the line slants upward from left to right, slants downward from left to right, or is horizontal?

2. The table below represents a linear relationship. Copy the table, and use the pattern to fill in the missing entries. Find the slope and the y-intercept of the graph of this relationship. Explain how you found your answers.

x	?	⁻6	⁻5	⁻4	⁻3	⁻2	⁻1	?	?
y	?	⁻10	⁻7	⁻4	⁻1	2	5	?	?

3. Confirm that the table below represents a linear relationship. What is the slope of the graph of this relationship?

x	46	47.1	48.1	49	50.1
y	31.5	34.14	36.54	38.7	41.34

As you work on these ACE questions, use your calculator whenever you need it.

Applications

In 1–4, find the slope and the y-intercept of the line represented by the equation.

1. $y = 10 + 3x$ **2.** $y = 0.5x$

3. $y = {}^-3x$ **4.** $y = {}^-5x + 2$

In 5–9, the table represents a linear relationship.

- Give the slope and the y-intercept of the graph of the relationship.
- Determine which of the following equations fits the relationship:

$y = 5 - 2x \quad y = 2x \quad y = {}^-3x - 2 \quad y = 2x - 1 \quad y = x + 3.5$

5.

x	0	1	2	3	4
y	0	2	4	6	8

6.

x	0	1	2	3	4
y	3.5	4.5	5.5	6.5	7.5

7.

x	0	1	2	3	4
y	$^-1$	1	3	5	7

8.

x	0	1	2	3	4
y	5	3	1	$^-1$	$^-3$

9.

x	1	2	3	4	5
y	$^-5$	$^-8$	$^-11$	$^-14$	$^-17$

In 10–13, find the slope of the line, and write an equation for the line.

10.

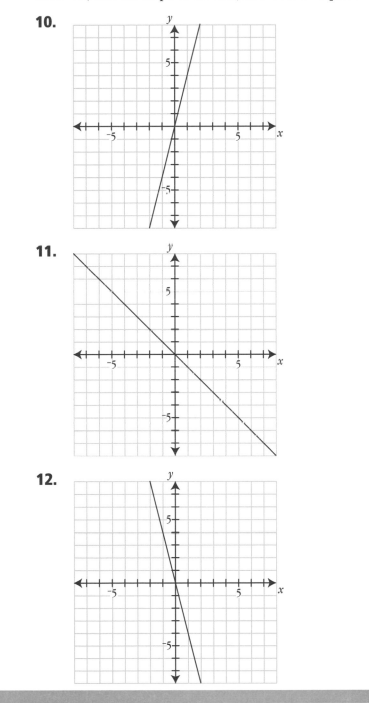

11.

12.

13.

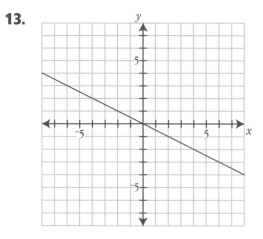

In 14–17, do parts a–d.

14. (0, 0) and (3, 3)   **15.** (⁻1, 1) and (3, ⁻3)

16. (0, ⁻5) and (⁻2, ⁻3)   **17.** (3, 6) and (5, 6)

    a. Plot the points on a coordinate grid, and draw a line through them.

    b. Find the slope of the line.

    c. Estimate the y-intercept from the graph.

    d. Use your answers from parts b and c to write an equation for the line.

In 18–20, do parts a–c.

18. $y = x$ **19.** $y = 2x + {}^-2$ **20.** $y = {}^-0.5x + 2$

    a. Make a table of x and y values for the equation.

    b. Make a graph of the equation.

    c. Find the slope of the graph.

In 21–23, determine which linear relationships in a–j fit the description.

21. The line for this relationship has positive slope.

22. The line for this relationship has a slope of ⁻2.

23. The line for this relationship has a slope of 0.

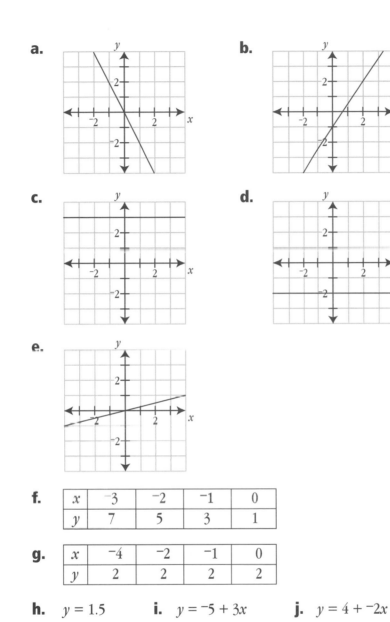

a.

b.

c.

d.

e.

f.

x	$^-3$	$^-2$	$^-1$	0
y	7	5	3	1

g.

x	$^-4$	$^-2$	$^-1$	0
y	2	2	2	2

h. $y = 1.5$ **i.** $y = {}^-5 + 3x$ **j.** $y = 4 + {}^-2x$

24. a. Find the slope of the line represented by the equation $y = x - 1$.

b. Make a table of x and y values for the equation $y = x - 1$. How is the slope related to the table entries?

25. a. Find the slope of the line represented by the equation $y = {}^-2x + 3$.

b. Make a table of x and y values for the equation $y = {}^-2x + 3$. How is the slope related to the table entries?

26. At noon, the temperature was 12°F. For the next 24 hours, the temperature fell by an average of 3°F an hour.

a. Write an equation for the temperature, T, n hours after noon.

b. What is the y-intercept of the line the equation represents? What does the y-intercept tell you about this situation?

c. What is the slope of the line the equation represents? What does the slope tell you about this situation?

27. Natasha never manages to make her allowance last for a whole week, so she borrows money from her sister. Suppose Natasha borrows 50 cents every week.

a. Write an equation for the amount of money, m, Natasha owes her sister after n weeks.

b. What is the slope of the graph of the equation from part a?

Connections

28. In Europe, many hills have signs indicating their steepness, or slope. Here are some examples:

 This means for each 4 meters in run the hill rises by 1 meter.

 This means for each 15 meters in run the hill falls by 1 meter.

On a coordinate grid, sketch hills with the above slopes.

29. In 1980, the town of Rio Rancho, located on a mesa outside Santa Fe, New Mexico, was destined for obscurity. But as a result of hard work by its city officials, it began adding manufacturing jobs at a fast rate. As a result, the city's population grew 239% from 1980 to 1990, making Rio Rancho the fastest-growing "small city" in the United States. The population of Rio Rancho in 1990 was 37,000.

   a. What was the population of Rio Rancho in 1980?

   b. If the same rate of population increase continues, what will the population be in the year 2000?

30. James and Janna share a veterinary practice. They each make farm visits two days a week. They take cellular phones on these trips to keep in touch with the office. James makes his farm visits on weekdays. His cellular phone rate is $14.95 a month plus $0.50 a minute. Janna makes her visits on Saturday and Sunday and is charged a weekend rate of $29.95 a month plus $0.25 a minute.

   a. Write an equation for each billing plan.

   b. Is it possible for James' cellular phone bill to be more than Janna's? Explain how you know this.

   c. Is it possible for James' and Janna's phone bills to be for the same amount? How many minutes of phone calls would each person have to make for their bills to be equal?

   d. Janna finds another phone company that offers one rate for both weekday and weekend calls. The billing plan for this company can be expressed by the equation $A = 25 + 0.25m$, where A is the total monthly bill and m is the number of minutes of calls. Compare this billing plan with the other two plans.

Extensions

31. **a.** Find the slope of each line below, and write an equation for the line.

i.

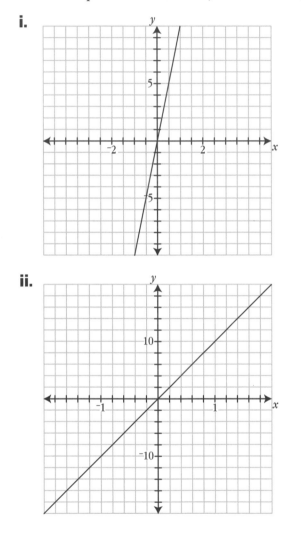

ii.

iii.

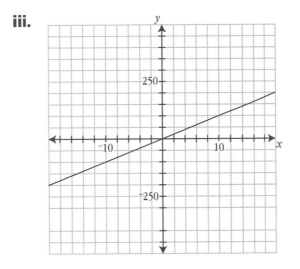

b. Compare the slopes of the three lines.

c. How are the three graphs similar? How are they different?

32. On a flight from Boston to Detroit last March, passengers were able to watch a monitor that gave the altitude and the outside temperature. Two middle school teachers on the flight decided to try to figure out a formula for the temperature, t, in degrees Fahrenheit at an altitude of a feet above sea level. One teacher said the formula is $t = 46 - 0.003a$, and the other said it is $t = 46 + 0.003a$.

a. Which formula makes more sense to you? Why?

b. The Detroit Metropolitan Airport is 620 feet above sea level. Use the formula you chose in part a to find the temperature at the airport.

c. Does the temperature you found in part b seem reasonable? Why or why not?

33. The graph below shows the altitude of a spaceship from 10 seconds before liftoff through 7 seconds after liftoff.

a. Describe the relationship between the altitude of the spaceship and time.

b. What is the slope for the part of the graph that is a straight line? What does this slope represent in this situation?

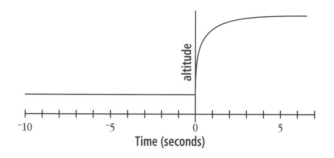

Mathematical Reflections

In this investigation, you learned about the slope, or steepness, of a line, and you discovered how to determine the slope from a table, a graph, or an equation. These questions will help you summarize what you have learned:

1. Explain what the slope of a line is.

2. How can you find the slope of a line from its equation? From its graph? From a table of values for the line? From the coordinates of two points on the line?

3. Describe how information about y-intercept and slope allows you to compare two equations. For example, how can you decide which equation has a steeper graph? How can you can you determine where the graphs of the equations cross the y-axis?

4. In *Comparing and Scaling*, you used ratios to make comparisons. What similarities are there between the way you used ratios in *Comparing and Scaling* and the way you have used slope in this unit?

Think about your answers to these questions, discuss your ideas with other students and your teacher, and then write a summary of your findings in your journal.

Writing an Equation for a Line

If you know the slope and the *y*-intercept of a line, it is easy to write an equation of the form $y = mx + b$ for the line. Unfortunately, you are not always given this information. How would you write an equation for a line if you knew only the coordinates of two points on the line? How would you write an equation for a line if you knew only the slope and the coordinates of a point that is not the *y*-intercept? In this investigation, you will work on some interesting problems in which you will consider questions like these.

6.1 Solving Alphonso's Puzzle

Today is Alphonso's birthday. Alphonso's grandfather gave Alphonso some money as a birthday gift. Alphonso says he will put his birthday money in a safe place and add part of his allowance to it each week. His sister Maria asks him how much his grandfather gave him and how much of his allowance he is planning to save each week. As usual, Alphonso does not answer his sister directly. Instead, he gives her some information and lets her puzzle out the answer for herself.

Problem 6.1

A. Alphonso tells Maria he will save the same amount from his allowance each week. He says that after five weeks he will have a total of $175 and after eight weeks he will have $190. How much money is Alphonso planning to save each week?

B. How much money did Alphonso's grandfather give him for his birthday?

■ Problem 6.1 Follow-Up
Write an equation for the total amount of money Alphonso will have saved after a given number of weeks. Describe the reasoning you used to write your equation.

6.2 Converting Temperatures

Detroit, Michigan, is just across the Detroit River from the Canadian city of Windsor, Ontario. Since Canada uses the Celsius temperature scale, weather reports in Detroit often give temperatures in both Fahrenheit and Celsius degrees. The relationship between Fahrenheit degrees and Celsius degrees is linear. In this problem, you will write an equation you can use to convert temperatures from one scale to the other.

Problem 6.2

Two important reference points for temperature are the boiling point and the freezing point of water. Water freezes at 0°C, or 32°F. Water boils at 100°C, or 212°F.

0°C, or 32°F   100°C, or 212°F

Use this information to write an equation for the relationship between Fahrenheit degrees and Celsius degrees.

■ Problem 6.2 Follow-Up

1. Find the y-intercept for the equation you wrote in Problem 6.2. What does the y-intercept tell you about this situation?

2. Find the slope for the equation you wrote in Problem 6.2. What does the slope tell you about this situation?

3. If it is 85°F outside, what is the Celsius temperature?

4. If it is 30°C outside, what is the Fahrenheit temperature?

6.3 Solving the Mystery of the Irish Elk

The data below were gathered by evolutionary
biologists studying an extinct animal called the
Irish elk. The Irish elk grew to sizes much larger
than any modern elk. The biologists were studying
fossils to try to find patterns that might help
them explain why this animal became extinct.

x	46	47.1	48.1	49	50.1
y	31.5	34.14	36.54	38.7	41.34

Source: *Ever Since Darwin*. Stephen Jay Gould. New York:
Norton, 1977. Data have been modified slightly.

The data are skull and antler measurements for
five different Irish elk fossils: x is the length of the
skull in centimeters, and y is the length of one
antler in centimeters.

In Problem 5.3 Follow-Up, you looked at the data in the above table. You showed that the
data are linear and found that the slope of the line that fits the data is 2.4. This means
that, for every 1-centimeter increase in the skull length, the antler length increases by
2.4 centimeters. You can use this information to write an equation that describes the
relationship between skull length and antler length. Your equation might give you clues
about why the Irish elk became extinct.

Problem 6.3

A. Since the relationship represented in the table is linear, its equation can be written in the form $y = mx + b$. You know the slope is 2.4, so the equation becomes $y = 2.4x + b$. Now you need to find the value of b, the y-intercept.

To find b, pick a pair of x and y values from the table, and substitute them into the equation

$$\square = 2.4\,\square + b$$

What value must b have? Substitute this value into $y = 2.4x + b$ to complete the equation.

B. Use your equation from part A to predict the antler length for a skull length of 55 centimeters.

C. For each Irish elk represented in the table, the antler length is shorter than the skull length. However, the Irish elk skeleton shown on page 82 has antlers much longer than its skull. Can you explain how the skull and antler data for this elk could fit the equation you wrote?

■ Problem 6.3 Follow-Up

1. Graph the data from the table on a coordinate grid. Use the graph to estimate the y-intercept. Do you get the same y-intercept you found in part A of Problem 6.3?

2. a. Use your graph to predict the antler length for a skull length of 55 centimeters. Do you get the same answer you got by using the equation? Explain.

b. Use the table to predict the antler length for a skull length of 55 centimeters. How does the result compare with the results you got by using the equation and the graph?

Did you know?

The Irish elk was not really an elk, and it wasn't exclusively Irish. It was actually a giant deer that inhabited parts of Europe, Asia, and northern Africa. The Irish elk evolved during the last million years and became extinct about 11,000 years ago. Fossils have been found showing that Irish elk had antlers with spreads of up to 12 feet! These antlers could not have been carried by any modern deer. Indeed, the antlers of the largest Irish elk are so out of proportion with the rest of the skeleton that biologists believe they were an encumbrance rather than an asset.

As you work on these ACE questions, use your calculator whenever you need it.

Applications

1. Write an equation for the line with slope ⁻3 and *y*-intercept 5.

2. Write an equation for the line with slope $\frac{3}{2}$ that passes through (0, 2).

3. Write an equation for the line that passes through (0, 1.5) and (1, 2.5).

4. Write an equation for the line that passes through (1, 5) and (4, 6).

5. Write an equation for the line that passes through (2, 6) and (3, 6).

In 6–9, write an equation for the line.

6.　　　　　　　　　　　　　　**7.**

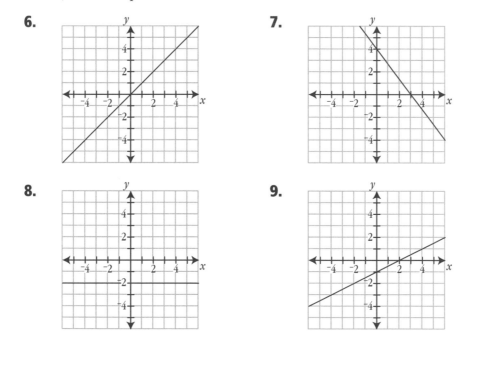

8.　　　　　　　　　　　　　　**9.**

In 10 and 11, write a linear equation that represents the data in the table.

10.

x	$^-1$	0	1	2	3
y	1	3	5	7	9

11.

x	1	2	3	4	5
y	3	2	1	0	$^-1$

12. On the Talk for Less long-distance phone plan, the relationship between the number of minutes a call lasts and the cost of the call is linear. A 5-minute call costs $1.25, and a 15-minute call costs $2.25.

    a. Write an equation for the relationship between the cost and the length of a call.

    b. Find the slope and the y-intercept for the equation, and explain what this information means in the context of this problem.

    c. How much will a 25-minute call cost?

    d. How long can a customer talk for $5.00?

13. The hardware store sells batteries individually. Five batteries cost $4.50, and seven batteries cost $6.30.

    a. Write an equation for the relationship between the cost and the number of batteries.

    b. Find the slope and the y-intercept for the equation, and explain what this information means in the context of this problem.

    c. How much do eight batteries cost?

    d. Dominique spent $10.80 on batteries. How many batteries did she buy?

14. Mr. Brock's class is planning a cookie sale to raise money for the local food bank. They took a survey to help them figure out how much to charge for each cookie. They found that the relationship between the price and the number of cookies they would sell is linear. According to the survey, they will sell about 200 cookies if they charge 50¢, and they will sell about 50 cookies if they charge $1.

    a. Write an equation for the relationship between the cost and the number of cookies.

    b. Find the slope and the *y*-intercept for the equation, and explain what this information means in the context of this problem.

    c. If they charge 70¢ for each cookie, about how many cookies will they sell?

    d. If they want to sell 300 cookies, how much should they charge?

15. You can figure out how far away lightning is by counting the number of seconds between a flash of lightning and the following clap of thunder. The speed of sound is about 1100 feet per second. Thus, if you hear thunder 3 seconds after you see lightning, the lightning hit about $3 \times 1100 = 3300$ feet away.

    a. Write an equation you can use to predict the distance lightning is from you from the number of seconds between the lightning and the thunder.

    b. Find the slope and the *y*-intercept for the equation, and explain what this information means in the context of this problem.

    c. If lightning hits 1 mile away, how many seconds will elapse before you hear the thunder?

    d. If you hear thunder $6\frac{1}{2}$ seconds after you see lightning, how far away did the lightning hit?

16. **a.** Describe a situation involving a linear relationship whose graph has the given slope.

      i. positive slope   **ii.** negative slope   **iii.** a slope of 0

    b. For each situation you described in part a, tell what information the slope and the *y*-intercept give about the situation.

Connections

17. The drawing below shows "trains" of triangles made from toothpicks.

Number of toothpicks	3	5	7
Number of triangles	1	2	3
Perimeter of train	3	4	5

    a. Write an equation for the relationship between the number of triangles in a train and the perimeter of the train. Check your equation by testing it on the next few trains in the pattern.

    b. Write an equation for the relationship between the number of triangles in a train and the number of toothpicks.

18. Repeat question 17 for trains of squares.

19. Repeat question 17 for trains of hexagons.

20. a. There is 0.62 mile in 1 kilometer. Write an equation for the relationship between miles and kilometers.

b. How many miles are in 15 kilometers?

c. How many kilometers are in 10 miles?

21. In January 1991, a huge oil slick appeared in the Persian Gulf. A couple of days after it was reported, it covered a rectangular area 50 kilometers long and 13 kilometers wide. One day later, it covered a rectangular area 57 kilometers long and 16 kilometers wide.

a. Assume that the area of the oil slick continued to change at the rate described above. What was the average rate of change of the area of the slick with respect to the number of days? Explain.

b. Assume the relationship between the area of the slick and time is linear. Write an equation that describes the area of the slick as a function of time.

c. Draw a graph showing the relationship between area and time.

d. Estimate how long the oil had been spreading at the time of the first report of its area.

e. Do you think the oil really spread at a constant rate? Why or why not?

22. The radius of a circular oil spill from a certain underwater drilling site grows at a rate of 10 feet per minute.

a. Use a table, a graph, and an equation to describe the growth of the radius of the spill over time.

b. Use a table, a graph, and an equation to describe the growth of the circumference of the spill over time.

c. Use a table, a graph, and an equation to describe the growth of the area of the spill over time.

d. Which of the relationships in parts a–c are linear? How did you decide?

23. The distance required to stop a car depends on the speed at which the car is traveling. This stopping distance can be divided into two parts. The *reaction distance* is the distance the car travels from the time the driver realizes there is a need to stop until she applies the brakes. The *braking distance* is the distance the car travels from the moment the brakes are applied until the car stops. The table below shows the reaction distance and the braking distance for travel at different speeds. The *total distance* is the sum of the reaction distance and the braking distance. Below the table, the graphs of reaction distance, braking distance, and total distance are shown on the same set of axes.

Speed (kilometers per hour)	0	20	40	60	80	100	120
Reaction distance (meters)	0	5	10	15	20	25	30
Braking distance (meters)	0	2.5	10	22	40	63	90
Total distance (meters)	0	7.5	20	37	60	88	120

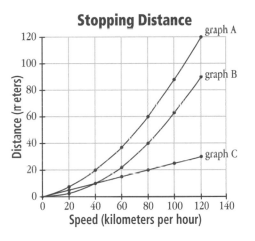

a. Which graph shows the relationship between reaction distance and speed?

b. Which graph shows the relationship between braking distance and speed?

c. Is either relationship linear? Explain your reasoning.

d. Match each equation with its graph.

 i. $d = 0.006s^2$ **ii.** $d = 0.25s$ **iii.** $d = 0.25s + 0.006s^2$

Extensions

24. Write an equation of the line that is parallel to the line $y = \frac{3}{2}x + 1$ and has a y-intercept of $(0, 3)$.

25. Write an equation of a line that is parallel to the line $y = 6$.

26. When Glenda travels in Europe, she uses a rule of thumb to convert Celsius temperatures to Fahrenheit temperatures: she doubles the Celsius temperature and adds $30°$.

    a. Write an equation for Glenda's rule of thumb.

    b. Convert a few Celsius temperatures to Fahrenheit temperatures, using both Glenda's rule of thumb and the equation you found in Problem 6.2. How do the results of the two conversion methods compare?

    c. Graph the equation for Glenda's rule and the equation from Problem 6.2 on the same set of axes.

    d. For what range of Celsius temperatures does Glenda's rule give Fahrenheit temperatures fairly close to those obtained by applying the equation from Problem 6.2?

27. Write an equation for a line that passes through the point $(3, {}^-3)$.

28. Write an equation for a line that passes through the point $(\frac{2}{3}, 4)$.

29. **a.** On a coordinate grid, draw a nonrectangular parallelogram, and write equations for the four lines that contain the sides of the parallelogram.

    b. On a coordinate grid, draw a rectangle, and write equations for the four lines that contain the sides of the parallelogram.

30. **a.** Repeat question 17 for trains of regular, eight-sided polygons.

    b. Repeat question 17 for trains of regular, ten-sided polygons.

    c. Can you make any generalizations about these equations for a figure with any number of sides?

Mathematical Reflections

In this investigation, you learned methods for finding an equation that fits given information. These questions will help you summarize what you have learned:

1. Explain how you can write an equation of a line from the given information. Use examples to illustrate your thinking.

   a. the slope and the y-intercept of the line

   b. two points on the line

   c. the slope of the line and a point on the line that is not the y-intercept

2. Why would you want to write an equation of a line? Use examples to illustrate your answer.

3. In this unit, you did a lot of work with equations. You wrote equations for linear relationships and then used the equations to find solutions and make predictions. Through your work, you probably developed ways to work efficiently with symbols. Apply what you learned to answer these questions.

   a. A student claims that $y = 3x + 10$ and $y = 10 + 3x$ are two ways to represent the same relationship. Do you agree? Why or why not? Can you think of some other ways to represent the relationship $y = 3x + 10$?

   b. What steps would you follow to find the value of y in $y = 10 + 3(^-4)$?

   Think about your answers to these questions, discuss your ideas with other students and your teacher, and then write a summary of your findings in your journal.

coefficient A number that is multiplied by a variable in an equation or expression. In a linear equation of the form $y = mx + b$, the number m is the coefficient of x *and* the slope of the line. For example, in the equation $y = 3x + 5$, the coefficient of x is 3. This is also the slope of the line.

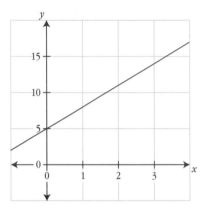

constant term A number in an equation that is not multiplied by a variable, or an amount added to or subtracted from the terms involving variables. In an equation of the form $y = mx + b$, the y-intercept, b, is a constant term. The effect of the constant term on a graph is to raise or lower the graph. The constant term in the equation $y = 3x + 5$ is 5. The graph of $y = 3x$ is raised vertically 5 units to give the graph of $y = 3x + 5$.

coordinate pair A pair of numbers of the form (x, y) that gives the location of a point in the coordinate plane. The x term gives the distance left or right from the origin $(0, 0)$, and the y term gives the distance up or down from the origin.

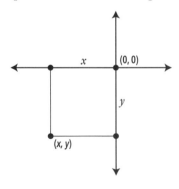

function A relationship between two variables in which the value of one variable depends on the value of the other variable. For example, the distance, d, in miles covered in t hours by a car traveling at 55 mph is given by the equation $d = 55t$. The relationship between distance and the time is a function, and we say that the distance is a *function of* the time. This function is a *linear function*, and its graph is a straight line whose slope is 5. In future units, you will learn about functions that are not linear.

intersecting lines Lines that cross or *intersect*. The coordinates of the point where the lines intersect are solutions to the equations for both lines. The graphs of the equations $y = x$ and $y = 2x - 3$ intersect at the point (3, 3). This number pair is a solution to each equation.

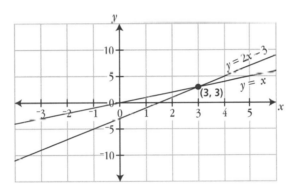

linear relationship A relationship in which there is a constant rate of change between two variables; for each unit increase in one variable, there is a constant change in the other variable. A linear relationship between two variables can be represented by a straight-line graph and by an equation of the form $y = mx + b$. The rate of change is m, the coefficient of x. For example, if you save \$2 each month, the relationship between the amount you save and the number of months is a linear relationship which can be represented by the equation $y = 2x$. The constant rate of change is 2.

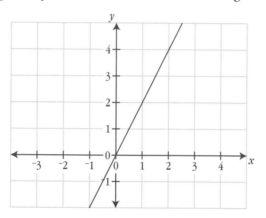

origin The point where the x- and y-axes intersect on a coordinate graph. With coordinates (0, 0), the origin is the center of the coordinate plane.

rise The vertical change between two points. The slope of a line is the rise divided by the run.

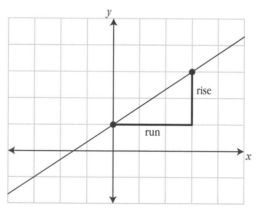

run The horizontal change between two points. The slope of a line is the rise divided by the run.

scale The distance between tick marks on the x- and y-axes of a coordinate grid. When graphing, an appropriate scale must be selected so that the resulting graph will be clearly shown. For example, when graphing the equation $y = 60x$, a scale of 1 for the x-axis and a scale of 15 or 30 for the y-axis would be reasonable.

slope The number that expresses the steepness of a line. The slope is the ratio of the vertical change to the horizontal change between any two points on the line. Sometimes this ratio is referred to as *the rise over the run*. The slope of a horizontal line is 0. Slopes are positive if the y values increase from left to right on a coordinate grid and negative if the y values decrease from left to right. The slope of a vertical line is undefined.

The slope of a line is the same as the constant rate of change between the two variables. For example, the points (0, 0) and (3, 6) lie on the graph of $y = 2x$. Between these points, the vertical change is 6 and the horizontal change is 3, so the slope is $\frac{6}{3} = 2$, which is the coefficient of x in the equation.

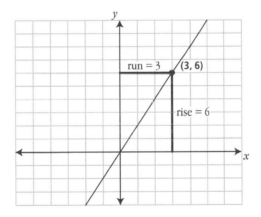

x-intercept The point where a graph crosses the *x*-axis. The *x*-intercept of the equation $y = 3x + 5$ is $(0, -\frac{5}{3})$ or $-\frac{5}{3}$.

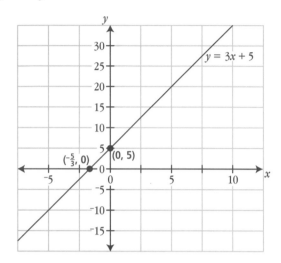

y-intercept The point where the graph crosses the *y*-axis. In a linear equation of the form $y = mx + b$, the *y*-intercept is the constant, *b*. In the graph above, the *y*-intercept is $(0, 5)$ or 5.